Children's Encyclopedia

igloo

This edition published in 2008
by Igloo Books Ltd
Cottage Farm
SywelL
NN6 0BJ
www.igloo-books.com

A copy of the British Library Cataloguing-in-Publication Data is available from the British Library

10 9 8 7 6 5 4 3 2 1

ISBN: 978 1 84817 251 7

Packaged by HL Studios, Long Hanborough, Oxon

Printed and manufactured in China

Introduction

This Children's Encyclopedia has been designed to help you to find interesting information quickly and easily. The topics are arranged in alphabetical order starting with Aardvark and finishing with Zoology with a whole variety of exciting topics in between.

If you're looking for information on a special topic for homework or for a project you should find lots to help you in these pages. You may just want to browse through the pages and see what topics you want to find out more about. Whatever you're looking for you're sure to find something in this encyclopedia.

We've enjoyed writing this for you and hope that you'll enjoy reading it!

Contents

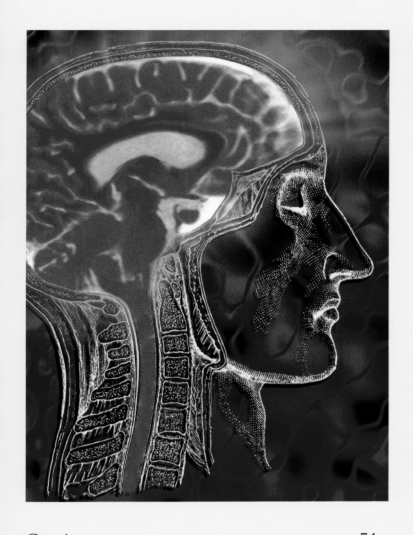

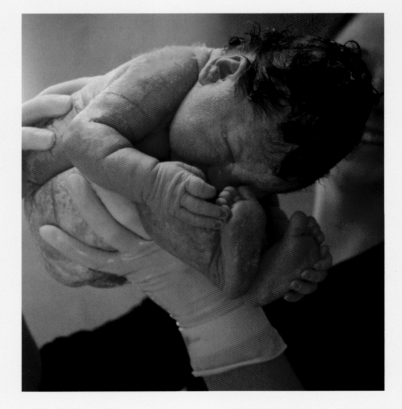

Famous astrologers: John Dee, Nostradamus, the Three Wise Men.

Astrology began to lose popularity as a science in the 17th century, when it became widely accepted that the Sun and not the Earth was the centre of the Universe.

When was the first horoscope made?

The earliest horoscope was made in 410 BC.

How do I know what my zodiac sign is?

Find your birthday. Check which sign covers that date.

Although millions of people can now read their daily horoscopes, at first horoscopes were only for royalty. Eventually the study of astrology was spread from the Babylonians to the Greeks, then later to the Romans and throughout the world.

Zodiac stones
Each zodiac sign has several 'birthstones' associated with it. Here are some of them:

Aries	amethyst, garnet, ruby, quartz
Taurus	peridot, jade, lapis lazuli, quartz
Gemini	agate, peridot, pearl, moonstone
Cancer	pearl, moonstone, sapphire, ruby, garnet
Leo	amber, diamond, topaz, ruby, garnet, peridot
Virgo	peridot, sapphire, aquamarine, blue topaz
Libra	blue topaz, aquamarine, rose quartz, opal, amethyst
Scorpio	rose quartz, opal, sapphire, topaz, smoky quartz
Sagittarius	amethyst, sapphire, topaz, smoky quartz, turquoise
Capricorn	onyx, garnet, turquoise, lapis lazuli
Aquarius	aquamarine, fossils, jet, garnet
Pisces	amethyst, aquamarine, bloodstone

Chinese astrology
The Chinese Zodiac is just as ancient as the Western one, and quite different. In traditional China, dating methods were cyclical – which means something that is repeated over and over again. The years on a Chinese calendar are grouped into sets of 12. Each year is assigned an animal name or 'sign' according to a repeating cycle. Therefore, every 12 years, the same animal sign would return.

Dog	1910, 1922, 1934, 1946, 1958, 1970, 1982, 1994, 2006
Boar	1911, 1923, 1935, 1947, 1959, 1971, 1983, 1995, 2007
Rat	1912, 1924, 1936, 1948, 1960, 1972, 1984, 1996
Ox	1913, 1925, 1937, 1949, 1961, 1973, 1985, 1997
Tiger	1914, 1926, 1938, 1950, 1962, 1974, 1986, 1998
Rabbit	1915, 1927, 1939, 1951, 1963, 1975, 1987, 1999
Dragon	1916, 1928, 1940, 1952, 1964, 1976, 1988, 2000
Snake	1917, 1929, 1941, 1953, 1965, 1977, 1989, 2001
Horse	1918, 1930, 1942, 1954, 1966, 1978, 1990, 2002
Goat	1919, 1931, 1943, 1955, 1967, 1979, 1991, 2003
Monkey	1920, 1932, 1944, 1956, 1968, 1980, 1992, 2004
Rooster	1921, 1933, 1945, 1957, 1969, 1981, 1993, 2005

Chinese astrologers believe you can tell what a person is like from the year they were born, as a person will have characteristics like those of the animal assigned to that year. For example, a person born in the Year of the Dragon is expected to be bold and successful. In the Chinese calendar, the beginning of the New Year falls somewhere between January and February, depending on the phases of the moon. At New Year, dancing and animal masks are used to welcome in the animal of the New Year.

Astronomy

Astronomy means to study the night sky and all of the stars, planets, moons, asteroids and meteors within it. It includes the whole universe, not just our own solar system. It's also about how the stars, moons and planets move around one another.

What is the Universe?

It is a huge wide-open space that holds everything from particles (minute pieces of matter – electrons or protons) to galaxies (enormous collections of gas, dust or stars). No one really knows just how big the Universe is. Astronomers try to measure it with an instrument called a spectroscope to tell whether an object is moving closer to the Earth or further away from it.

Galaxies

There are billions of galaxies in the Universe. Some galaxies are called 'spiral', because they look like giant pinwheels in the sky. The galaxy we live in, the Milky Way, is a spiral galaxy. Some galaxies are called 'elliptical', because they look like flat balls. A galaxy may be called 'irregular' if it doesn't really have a shape. A new type of galaxy was discovered recently, called a 'starburst' galaxy. In this type of galaxy, new stars just seem to 'burst out' very quickly.

The Milky Way

This is the galaxy that our solar system belongs to. It is over 100,000 light-years wide. A light-year is a unit of distance. It is the distance that light can travel in one year. One light-year is equal to 9,500 billion km (5,900 billion miles). It is a spiral galaxy because it has long arms which spin around like a giant pinwheel. Our Sun is a star in one of the arms. When you look up at the night sky, most of the stars you see are in one of the Milky Way arms. It is known as the Milky Way because the ancient Romans called it the Via Galactica, or 'road made of milk'.

Fascinating facts

Scientists believe that billions of years ago there was a powerful explosion called the Big Bang. This explosion set the Universe into motion and this motion continues today.

Stars twinkle because we see them through thick layers of turbulent (moving) air in the Earth's atmosphere. Stars would not appear to twinkle if we viewed them from outer space or from a planet/moon that didn't have an atmosphere!

Stars

Stars are held together by gravity. There may be millions, or even billions, of stars in one galaxy.

Stars use a lot of energy, which produces light. Small stars will shrink after they've used up their power and will become a 'white dwarf'. A 'white dwarf' is a star that has used up its original hydrogen and helium fuel and has shrunk in size. It shines with heat that is left over.

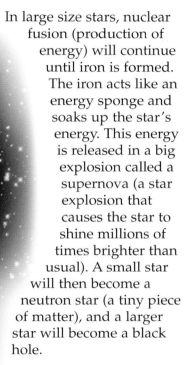

In large size stars, nuclear fusion (production of energy) will continue until iron is formed. The iron acts like an energy sponge and soaks up the star's energy. This energy is released in a big explosion called a supernova (a star explosion that causes the star to shine millions of times brighter than usual). A small star will then become a neutron star (a tiny piece of matter), and a larger star will become a black hole.

Black holes

It's very hard to see a black hole. Black holes were once massive stars that used up all their power. As they died out their gravity made them collapse. Any object that gets too close to a black hole will be pulled inside it. We know they are there because of the effect they have on other objects that are near them. Any object (dust or a star) that gets too close to a black hole will be pulled inside it. As the objects fall toward the black hole, they heat up and get very hot. Scientists can use special instruments to measure the heat the objects give off.

How big is a galaxy?

A typical spiral galaxy in the constellation **Coma Berenices** *is about 56,000 light-years in diameter.*

What is an astronomer?

An astronomer is a person who studies the planets and stars. They use very sophisticated equipment, such as radio telescopes.

Australia

Australia is the largest island on the continent of Australia Oceania. Native Australians have inhabited it for over 42,000 years. European explorers and traders starting arriving in the 17th century and in the 18th century the British claimed part of the eastern half of the continent as a penal (prison) colony. This area became known as New South Wales. The population grew and eventually five more states were successively established over the course of the 19th century.

These were Victoria, Queensland, Northern Territory, Western Australia and South Australia. The island to the south of the mainland is Tasmania. On 1 January 1901, the six colonies became a federation and the Commonwealth of Australia was formed.

After the Second World War the Australian government promoted an immigration programme: over half of the migrants were British; others were Greek, German, Dutch, Italian and Yugoslav. Today over 90% of the population are of European descent; others are from Asia and the Middle East. Over 150 nationalities are represented in the population.

What is a flying doctor?

Australians living in the outback can be far from the nearest town. The Flying Doctor service started in 1928 to provide emergency health care.

Was Tasmania once joined to Australia?

Yes, it is believed that the island was joined to the mainland until the end of the most recent ice age, about 10,000 years ago.

Canberra is Australia's capital, but Sydney is its largest city and commercial centre, as well as having the world famous opera house and the 503 m (1,650 ft) long Sydney Harbour Bridge – which has eight lanes of roadway, two railway tracks, a cycle track and a walkway.

Sydney Opera House

The world's fussiest eater is the koala, which feeds exclusively on eucalyptus leaves. It eats only six of the 500 species of eucalyptus.

Although hunters have used throwing sticks in many parts of the world, the most famous of all such weapons is the Aborigine's boomerang, which may be the world's only returning throwing stick.

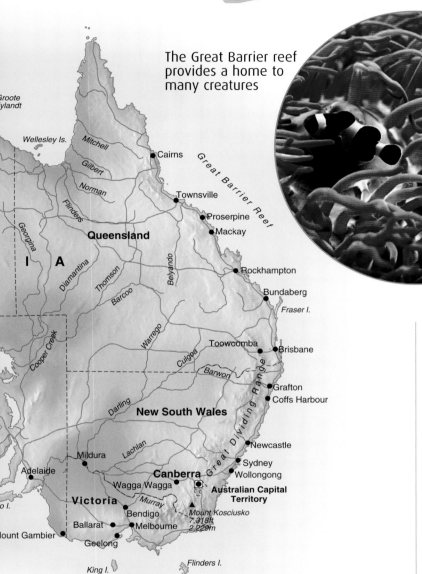

The Great Barrier reef provides a home to many creatures

Climate

While a large proportion of inland Australia is desert, 40% of the country enjoys a tropical climate. Snow falls in the Australian Alps at the south end of the Great Dividing Range, or Eastern Highlands. This is Australia's most substantial range of mountains, which stretches from north-eastern Queensland into the central plain in western Victoria.

The Great Barrier Reef

The Great Barrier Reef, situated off the coast of Queensland, is the world's longest reef, stretching 2,000 km (1,243 miles). It is a breeding ground for green and loggerhead turtles and home to humpback whales and dolphins. Among the many fish that inhabit Australia's surrounding waters are sharks, rays and lungfish. The lungfish is unusual because it has lungs as well as a gill-breathing system.

The Reef is under threat from the crown-of-thorns starfish which eats the living coral, and also from rising sea levels and tourism, which damage the fragile coral ecosystem.

Isolated communities

The Alice Springs School of the Air provides an educational service for children living in settlements and covers over 1 million sq km (386,000 sq miles) of central Australia. These children live in an isolated environment and their school classes were conducted via shortwave radio until very recently. Today most schools use wireless Internet links to receive their lessons.

Native Australians

The native Australians, known as Aborigines, were the first inhabitants of Australia. The term Aborigine includes a number of native peoples throughout Australia Oceania. These native Australians were hunter-gatherers; this means that they moved from place to place in search of food. They had no permanent buildings.

When the Europeans arrived they brought disease with them, and many of the native people died from illnesses such as smallpox. Today, many have abandoned their traditional tribal way of life and live in towns and cities, making up 1.5% of the population.

The regional headquarters of the flying doctor service in Queensland

The Aztecs

The Aztecs were the last native American rulers of Mexico. Around the end of the 12th century, their wandering tribe left its home in the north and settled in the Valley of Mexico, which they called 'Anahuac'. Here they built their capital city, Tenochtítlan. Over the next 200 years, the Aztecs built a powerful empire of around 12 million people.

Tenochtítlan

In Tenochtítlan the Aztecs built awe-inspiring temples and giant pyramids where they sacrificed captured prisoners to their gods by cutting out their hearts. They had a mighty army and grew rich by collecting tributes (payments) from all the tribes they conquered.

The fall of the Aztec Empire

The great Aztec Empire came to an end suddenly. In 1519, when Aztec civilisation was at its height, Spanish explorers ('conquistadors') arrived in Mexico led by a man named Hernán Cortés. The Spanish made war on the Aztecs and defeated them. The last independent Aztec Emperor, Montezuma II, was captured by the Spanish and killed. The Aztec Empire crumbled and the Spanish invaders took over.

Aztec jade mask

The Aztec gods

As farmers, the Aztecs depended heavily on the forces of nature and worshipped many of them as gods. Their chief god was Huitzilopochtli, the sun god and god of war. Other gods worshipped were Tlaloc (the god of rain), Quetzalcoatl the Feathered Serpent (the god of wind and learning), and Tezcatlipoca the Smoking Mirror (god of the night sky). The Aztecs believed they had to keep their 'good' gods strong by making human sacrifices to them – if they failed to do this, they believed other 'evil' gods would destroy the world. The Aztec priests used stone-bladed knives to cut out the hearts of up to 1,000 people a week and offer them to the sun god. Most of the people sacrificed were captured war prisoners, though Aztec warriors would sometimes volunteer for the most important rituals – they believed it was a great honour to be chosen. According to legend, in 1487 Aztec priests sacrificed more than 80,000 prisoners of war at the dedication of the rebuilt temple of the sun god!

The Aztecs built elaborate water systems for their cities

Art and writing
The Aztecs wrote in small pictures called 'pictographs'. This form of writing was very difficult to learn and was mainly done by priests or scribes.

The Aztecs made wonderful jewellery using gold, silver, copper, emerald, turquoise and jade (they prized jade above all other materials). They also fashioned vividly-dyed cloth, dramatic stone sculptures and elaborate garments made of the feathers of tropical birds.

The story of Tenochtitlán

At first, the Aztecs were a poor, ragged people, driven from place to place. Then their leader, Tenoch, had a vision. The sun god Huitzilopochtli told him to lead his people to a swampy island in the middle of Lake Texcoco. There he should look for an eagle perched on a cactus, eating a serpent. On that spot, they were to build their city. The city they built in about 1325 was named Tenochtitlán ('the city of Tenoch') and was built on one natural and several artificial islands in the swampy lake. The Aztecs built bridges and causeways to connect the city to the mainland, and canals to enable people to move around easily. The city quickly grew from a collection of mud huts and small temples to the capital city of a mighty empire – by 1519 about 60,000 people lived or did business there. Today Mexico City stands in the same place.

Maize

Stone knife, used for human sacrifices

Q&A?

Did the Aztecs play musical instruments?

Yes, especially during religious ceremonies. The most common instruments were rattles, whistles, trumpets, flutes, copper bells, and shells.

What did the Aztecs eat?

Corn was their main crop. Women ground the corn into coarse flour to make flat corn cakes called tortillas, which were their principal food. Other crops included beans, chilli peppers, squash, avocadoes and tomatoes.

Two calendars

The Aztecs had two calendars, a religious one and a solar one. The religious calendar told them when to consult their gods. The solar calendar was used to fix the best time for planting crops. A religious year had 260 days. A solar year had 365 days – 18 months of 20 days each and 5 'spare' days.

Stone solar calendar

Butterflies *and* moths

Butterflies are among the most colourful and beautiful types of insect on our planet. Both butterflies and moths belong to the Lepidoptera group of insects. We tend to see more butterflies as they are generally active during the day, whereas moths tend to be seen more at night.

The life cycle of a butterfly

The life cycle of all butterflies and moths has four distinct stages: starting as an egg, then caterpillar (larva), pupa (chrysalis) to the final stage of imago (adult). The process of change from one stage to the next is called metamorphosis. The final three stages of the Monarch butterfly (caterpillar, pupa and butterfly) are shown above.

How do butterflies keep safe from their predators?

With their wings closed, butterflies face the sun so that their shadow is small and predators are less likely to notice them.

How do butterflies get their energy?

Butterflies spread their wings out in the sunshine to soak up the warmth which gives them energy to fly.

Most butterflies and moths live only a few weeks although some, such as Red Admirals, will find somewhere sheltered to hibernate (sleep) during the winter before emerging again in warmer weather in the spring. During their short lives they all have to find a mate and lay eggs ready to become the next generation before they die.

Female butterflies and moths lay their eggs on plants. Each type of caterpillar has a particular type of plant which it prefers so the eggs will be laid on these plants ready to provide it with food as it hatches. Caterpillars have very strong jaws which they use to cut themselves

Monarch
butterfly

Green veined
white butterfly

out of their egg and escape from their shell which they then eat before going on to eat plant matter. The caterpillar's hard jaw contains a tough substance called chitin. As the caterpillar grows it sheds its skin (moults) as it outgrows it. When it reaches the stage of its final moult the caterpillar stops eating and finds a sheltered place to pupate which means that it changes into a pupa or chrysalis.

Some caterpillars spin a cocoon around themselves whilst others wrap themselves in rolled-up leaves. As a pupa the caterpillar undergoes the transformation into a butterfly or moth. This process takes several weeks. Once the adult is ready to emerge it gradually spreads out its wings pumping blood into them as they expand and dry. The adult is then ready to fly and begin the life cycle all over again.

Many types of butterfly and moth are now extinct or in danger of extinction. This has happened because they have been caught, collected and displayed for their beauty or because their natural habitats (where they live) have been destroyed by farming or building.

Butterfly wings are covered with shiny, coloured scales which reflect the light, shimmering as they fly.

Peacock butterflies have circles on their wings which look like eyes and are designed to frighten their enemies and so protect them from danger.

The ragged edge and brown colouring of a Comma butterfly enables it to look like a dead leaf on the ground.

fascinating
Facts

Elephant hawk moth

Cameras *and* photography

The word camera comes from the Latin *camera obscura* meaning 'dark chamber'. A camera obscura is a dark box with a hole in one side, so that light projects an upside-down image onto the opposite end of the box. In the past this was sometimes done with a whole dark room – people would stand inside it to view the image!

Pinhole cameras

The simplest type of camera is like a camera obscura and called a pinhole camera. It is a small, light-tight can or box with a black interior and a tiny hole in the centre of one end. The end opposite the pinhole is flat so that film or photographic paper can be held flat against it. The pinhole has a cover to stop light entering the camera when you are not taking a picture. It was used in the 16th century as an artist's tool. It did not use film but just projected the image onto a piece of paper.

How do cameras work?

Other cameras are more complicated versions of these earlier models and use a lens instead of a hole. Lenses (discovered in the late 13th century) are pieces of curved glass that magnify – make bigger – the image and concentrate the incoming light. Opposite the lens is a light-sensitive surface, either film or, in digital cameras, an imaging device. When you take a photograph, light reflects off the object being viewed, through the lens and onto the light-sensitive surface. White objects reflect the most light and black reflect the least, changing the material in different amounts and leaving an image. Photographic film is developed in a darkroom using chemicals that bring out and 'fix' the image.

The subjects of early photos had to sit very still – sometimes up to five minutes

Early photographic prints

Experiments were made in the 18th and early 19th centuries to try to make a lasting print from the image viewed. Several people discovered ways to do this. In 1826, Josephe Nicéphore Niépce recorded a negative on paper. (A negative is where the image is reversed, so that dark appears light and light appears dark.) He used light-sensitive chemicals on paper. Where the light fell on the paper, the chemical created a dark area, which led to the negative. William Fox-Talbot patented his calotype process in 1841. This process involved using light-sensitive paper to produce a negative, then soaking the image in a bath of sodium thiosulphate to 'fix it'. In 1839 Louis Jacques Mandé Daguerre 1839 invented a method for making positive prints on a silver plate.

The wet-plate process

The popularity of photography exploded when a new wet-plate process was invented. It combined detail with the ability to make multiple prints. There was great demand for family portraits and all kinds of other pictures. Photographers travelled to far-off lands, bringing back pictures of new animals and tribal peoples. Scientists used stop-action photography to show, for the very first time, how animals moved!

When was the camera obscura first used?

Although the first drawing we have of a camera obscura is by Leonardo Da Vinci in the 16th century, the ancient Greeks used this device to view solar eclipses safely!

What is the earliest surviving photograph?

The earliest known surviving photograph is an outdoor scene taken by Niépce in 1826 or 1827. Niépce called his process 'heliography', meaning 'sun writing'. It was a slow process which required about eight hours of bright sunlight!

The dry-plate process

In 1871 the dry-plate process was invented. This was easier and faster than the wet-plate and meant pictures did not need to be developed on the spot in mobile darkrooms.

An instant Polaroid camera

This new process and the invention of smaller cameras meant photo-journalists were able to go to many new places, bringing back pictures for newspapers and magazines. Documentary photography became popular, recording how people lived and also wars. Photography began to be accepted not just as an aid to the painter, but as an art form in itself!

Roll film

In 1888 George Eastman introduced roll film (replacing individual plates) and began to sell roll-film cameras. Now people could easily take pictures themselves. There were many developments like portable lights, colour film and Polaroid film, which created a finished print in seconds.

Modern cameras

Over the years cameras have become smaller, lighter and easier to use. Recently digital cameras have become popular, and many people even have cameras on their mobile phones! Digital photography allows people to make prints very easily and store their photographs on computers or send them to friends and family by email.

Compact digital camera

Photography today

Nowadays photography is available to us all and we are surrounded by images from all over the world. Photography has had a huge effect on business, education and journalism. The police use photographs to record crime scenes and even recognise criminals. Advanced cameras are also used in science, astronomy and medicine, allowing people to see the far-off stars and even the insides of living human beings!

Single lens reflex (SLR) camera

fascinating facts

The word photography comes from the Greek words for light and writing. The earliest surviving photograph dates from 1826. Daguerreotypes were made with toxic mercury!

Castles

When we use the word 'castle', we most often mean a self-contained fortress built to defend against enemies and control the area around it. Besides being used for protection, castles sometimes served as residences for the lord or monarch. During the Middle Ages, feudal lords who wanted to protect their people and expand their power built large numbers of castles all over Europe.

Early castles

The first castles were constructed of wood and so were easily destroyed by fire. Later castles were built of stone and were therefore much more robust. Many early stone castles consisted of a single tower. As time went on, however, castles became bigger, more elaborate and better designed for defence. Many of these castles survive today.

Where were castles built?

When possible, castles were built in places that were easy to defend, such as hills, mountain passes, peninsulas, and islands in lakes. They were often built to protect important strategic places such as ports and river crossings. For example, Stirling Castle in Scotland is built at a cross of the River Forth.

Castle design

Most castles had a keep, or central tower. The keep usually had several floors and included lodgings for the lord and perhaps his family and other important people. Castles usually had outer walls – sometimes several layers of them! – to provide the first line of defence when the castle was attacked. If the walls were breached (broken through), the people in the castle

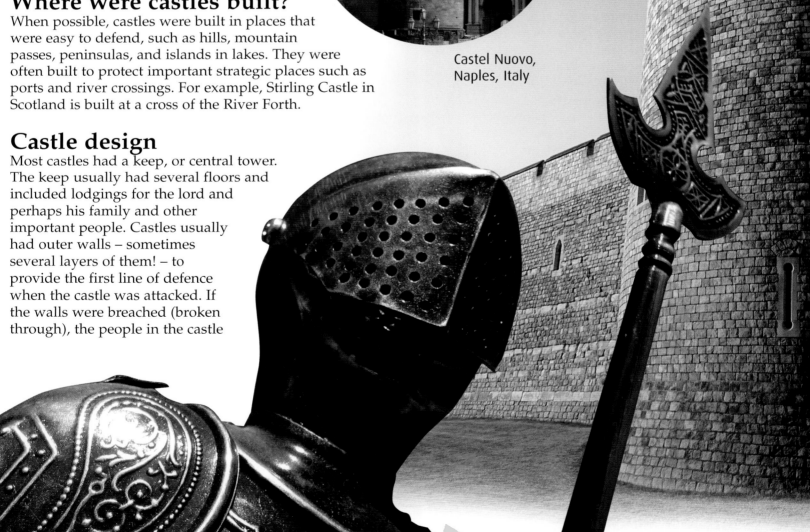

Castel Nuovo, Naples, Italy

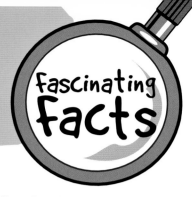

Many English castles were destroyed or badly damaged during the Civil War of the 17th century because Oliver Cromwell wanted to remove all traces of royal power.

The word dungeon comes from the French word *donjon*, meaning tower or keep. Prisoners in medieval castles were more often held in the highest room of a tower than in what we would now call a 'dungeon'.

could retreat into the keep. When many people needed protection, walls could be built around a whole city or town (for example, Carcassonne in France). In addition to the outer walls, castles had towers and battlements from which to watch for enemies. Castles with round towers were more difficult to attack because rocks bounced off the curved walls.

A crenellated wall

Castles under siege

When the castle was under attack it was said to be 'under siege'. Attackers would try many different ways to take over the castle. They would climb the walls or break them down by throwing heavy rocks at them, using machines such as catapults. Battering rams would be used to try to break down the gates. If a siege went on for a long time the attackers might try to starve out those who lived there by ensuring that no new supplies could get in.

Defending a castle

Inside the castle defenders would have a good view of their attackers from the high battlements and towers and would use bows and arrows to keep them away. There were often small slits so that archers could fire their arrows without being hit themselves. If attackers got close to the castle and put tall ladders up the walls, those inside would pour boiling water and hot sand onto them from the tops of the walls to keep them away. After the invention of gunpowder in the 13th century, however, defending a castle became harder and harder.

Castles since the Middle Ages

By the late 1600s, gunpowder and artillery had become so effective that castles were no longer useful for defence. As life became more peaceful, many of the castles that still survived were used for other purposes. For example, in the Scottish highlands, castles were often used as courts to settle disputes that were presided over by the laird. Others, such as the Tower of London and the Bastille in Paris, were used as prisons. Today many castles survive as monuments to the past, and large numbers of people visit them every year.

Q&A?

What is the 'iron ring' of castles?

This is a series of strong stone castles built in Wales by King Edward I (1239–1307) to control the Welsh population. They include the castles of Caernarfon, Harlech and Conwy.

Where does the word 'castle' come from?

It comes from the Latin word castellum, *meaning fortress. The word* castrum, *used for the wooden forts built by Roman soldiers, means a fortified place.*

Codes *and* code-breaking

Codes have been used throughout history to send important secret messages or to keep them short. Codes and ciphers are not the same. A message in code has words, phrases, or messages replaced by different words, letters, or symbols. Writing a message in code is called encoding. Ciphers, on the other hand, replace every single letter, number, or symbol with a different letter, number, or symbol. Writing a message using this method is called enciphering.

The two kinds of cipher

There are two main types of cipher. The first is called a 'transposition' cipher, when the letters of a message are scrambled up following a system that allows the message to be unscrambled by the receiver. For example, 'codesorciphers' (codes or ciphers) might become 'ocedoscrpiehsr'. Here each pair of letters has been reversed. So 'co' becomes 'oc', 'de' becomes 'ed' and so on. The second type is called a 'substitution' cipher. This is when letters are substituted for other letters or words for other words, for example, 'xe' being written for the letter 'j' or 'cabbage' being written for the word 'house'. This is what is most commonly meant when people say someone is talking 'in code',: 'did you buy some butter?' being the secret code for 'we attack at dawn'.

Ciphers in history

Ciphers are essential in times of war as a message written in normal language would be easily understood by the enemy and give away military secrets. People throughout history, including Julius Caesar and Mary, Queen of Scots, have used codes and ciphers. Military messages are sent in code between camps of soldiers or from generals to their troops. Other groups of people in history have also used secret codes to communicate with each other. Early Christians would draw a fish to tell other Christians who they were, and tramps in the 19th century would chalk secret symbols onto houses to let other tramps know that the inhabitants would either give a good meal or were unfriendly.

Breaking enemy codes

The military often employs cryptographers to study enemy ciphers. A common way to 'break' a code is to look at what words, symbols or combinations of letters turn up most frequently in the message. In English, the most common letters are E, T, O, A, N (in that order) and the most common combinations are TH, HE, IN, AN. This is called 'frequency analysis' and was discovered as a reliable method for breaking early transposition ciphers as early as the year 1000. Even complex codes are still vulnerable to this method as it is still possible to spot frequent letters and to use them to solve the puzzle.

'Code-talkers'

During World War One many Native American languages were used for the sending of secret messages because these languages were spoken by only a very few people. Following this, Navajo 'code-talkers' were used in important US missions in World War Two. This tribal language was an extremely complex and unwritten language with no alphabet. The code-talkers used the language itself but also a substitution cipher. Seemingly unrelated words stood for letters of the alphabet, for example the Navajo words for ant, abacus, alphabet, and apple would all stand for the letter 'a'. Other words and phrases were given special code-words, for example the word for 'hummingbird' meant 'fighter plane'. The code was never cracked.

How does Morse code work?

Morse code is made up of 'dots' and 'dashes'. A dot is a short tap of the telegraph key (or flash of the lamp) and a dash is three times longer.

What is 'Semaphore'?

Semaphore is a famous code that uses a pair of flags in different positions to spell out words.

Machines and cryptography

The most famous cipher machine was the German 'Enigma' machine used in World War Two. This machine encoded a message several times over instead of just once, and the parts which set the code, called the rotating discs, were changed daily, thus making the code even harder to solve

The British captured one of these machines and used mathematicians to break the codes. The very first computers were invented and built to help solve the code. They were so large that they filled a whole room!

Computers have meant that much more complicated ciphers can be invented, but it is also possible to use computers to break codes.

Enigma machine

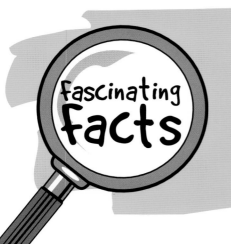

International Morse code was very useful in helping ships communicate quickly and for sending distress signals. The US Coastguard only stopped monitoring Morse code transmissions in 1995!

The *International Code of Signals* was compiled by the British Government in 1857 to be used by boats. This code uses different colours and shapes of flags to represent letters and numbers.

Telegraph key used to transmit Morse code

Desert life

A desert is a region that receives an annual rainfall of less than 250 mm (10 inches). The people and animals that live in desert areas must adapt to the conditions to survive. People like the Bedouins usually live in groups and move from place to place with the animals. Where there are homes in the desert, the houses usually have flat roofs and small windows. Whereas most animals need to have regular access to water, camels can survive for a week without water.

Deserts are generally rocky and bare and only partly covered in sand. Where there are large amounts of sand, the strong wind in sandstorms blows it into huge piles making sand dunes. It can then be very difficult for people to find their way as the landscape is constantly changing.

Desert plants

Plants which are found in deserts need very long roots to reach water underground, or thick stems which soak up water. Cacti can store water inside their stems and the whole plant swells up when it rains. In less severe conditions plants with leaves are often pale grey to reflect the light, and need very little water to grow. Seeds lie dormant during dry periods and grow and bloom and produce new seed very quickly when the rains come. In some places there are oases in deserts, where there is water. Palm trees often grow around an oasis.

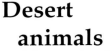
Cactus

Desert animals

Many animals live in deserts, although they are rarely seen. As deserts are normally very hot during the day and very cold at night, most animals will only come out to hunt and find food at the cooler times of day, early in the morning or in the evening. Most desert animals are specially adapted to cope with desert life. Fennec foxes have huge over-sized ears to help them lose body heat quickly and easily. Sand grouse are very pale in colour, so well camouflaged and difficult to spot among the rocks.

Sand grouse

 **How many sorts of camels are there?**

There are two types of camel: dromedary and Bactrian. The majority of the world's camels – about 15 million worldwide – are dromedaries with one fatty hump on their back where they store fluid. The less numerous camel is the Bactrian or Asian camel, which has a shaggier coat and two humps.

Llama

How is sand made?

The extremes of temperature in deserts mean that the rocks are continually expanding and contracting in the heat of the day and cold of the night. This causes the surface of rocks to break off into tiny fragments, which become sand. As the sand is blown about, new rock surfaces are exposed and the process continues.

There are deserts on every continent on Earth. They are the driest places in the world and sometimes there is no rain for many years.

Llamas, which come from South America, are closely related to camels. They are also traditionally used for carrying goods and for their meat. Llamas are smaller than camels, weighing about 150 kg and measuring just over a metre in height.

Camels

How can camels go so long without water when other animals cannot? Although camels don't have to drink very often, perhaps only once a week, when they do drink they can consume as much as 100 litres at a time. That would be the same sort of quantity as half a tank of petrol in your family car.

Camels are often called 'ships of the desert' as they are used for carrying people and heavy loads of supplies across deserts. They are also used for the milk, meat and skin which they provide. Camels can grip very thorny food from plants with their tough lips and large teeth. In a sandstorm they protect themselves by pressing their ears flat, closing their eyes and sealing their mouths and nostrils almost completely. In this way they avoid breathing in sand or getting it in their eyes, which are protected by very long eyelashes.

Lizard on cactus

Camel

Which is the world's largest desert?

The world's largest desert is the Sahara Desert in northern Africa. The Sahara covers nearly 10 million square kilometres (4 million square miles).

Dinosaurs

The word dinosaur comes from the Greek word *dino* (terrible) and the Latin word *saurus* (lizard). Although dinosaurs became extinct (died out) millions of years ago, we know that they existed because we have discovered dinosaur fossils. A fossil is an animal or plant that has been preserved for millions of years. A cast forms when mud and stones are deposited on animal or plant remains and, over millions of years, they turn to stone. Sometimes whole insects or plants are covered in amber or ice, so that they are perfectly preserved.

Early developments

The first dinosaur fossils were found a few hundred years ago. In 1822 an English couple, Mary Ann and Gideon Mantell, found what they thought to be the teeth of some huge, extinct iguana. Then, in 1841, the British scientist Sir Richard Owen realised that these bones were not those of any creature living at the time. In 1842 he gave these ancient creatures the name 'dinosaurs'.

Fossil

The 'Bone Wars'

Early palaeontology, which is the study of fossils or extinct plants and animals, was often based more on guesswork than true scientific evidence. This situation was improved when two rival and wealthy Americans, Othniel Marsh and Edward Cope, raced to excavate fossils in the Rocky Mountain region. In the late 1800s, their separate teams, armed against Native Americans and each other, dug up tons of bones from several sites. All in all, Marsh and Cope's rivalry (the 'Bone Wars') uncovered 136 new species. And their fossil displays created a huge interest in dinosaurs all around the world.

Fascinating Facts

The earliest dinosaur known to have existed was the *Eoraptor*, a meat eater that lived about 228 million years ago.

Micropachycephalosaurus (tiny thick-headed lizard) has the longest name of any dinosaur, but it is one of the smallest ever discovered – it was only about 0.5–1 m (1.5–3 ft) long!

How many different kinds of dinosaur were there?

There were more than 500 kinds that we know of, and more are still being discovered!

What does the name 'Mesozoic' mean?

It means 'middle animals'.

Discovering dinosaur species

The first dinosaur species to be discovered was *Iguanadon*, in 1822. Two years later, 1824, *Megalosaurus* was discovered. Dinosaurs have been discovered all over the world. For example, *Ankylosaurus* was discovered in Antarctica! Feathered dinosaurs have been found in China, making people think there might be a link between birds and dinosaurs. *Tyrannosaurus Rex* (left) was discovered in 1902.

What were dinosaurs like?

Until William Parker Foulke discovered the dinosaur Hadrosaurus in 1888, scientists had believed that dinosaurs were quadrupedal (walked on four legs) like modern lizards. However, Hadrosaurus, the first nearly complete dinosaur ever discovered, was clearly bipedal (walked on two legs). Some dinosaurs were herbivores (plant eaters), for example, Triceratops, and some were carnivores (meat eaters), for example, Tyrannosaurus Rex. Scientists think that smaller dinosaurs like Velociraptor were fast moving and bigger ones like Ankylosaurus were slow moving.

When did dinosaurs live?

Dinosaurs lived during the *Mesozoic* period of Earth's history, sometimes known as the 'Age of Reptiles'. They lived on earth for more than 165 million years but suddenly became extinct 65 million years ago. There have been many suggestions for why they became extinct, but scientists think that the most likely cause was an asteroid hitting the earth, causing huge changes in Earth's weather and temperature to which the dinosaurs couldn't adapt.

Electricity

Electricity usually means either an electric current, which is the flow of tiny electrically charged particles, or static electricity, a build-up of electrically charged particles in an object. We can easily convert electricity into other forms of energy such as heat and light.

Thomas Edison gave us one of the most familiar sights in our homes today when he perfected the light bulb in 1879, and since then we have developed hundreds of uses for electricity.

Electric current and circuits

Electric current is the flow of electric charge through a material. If electricity can flow easily through a material then that material is called a conductor, if it is difficult for electrical charge to move through a material then it is called an insulator. Most metals are very good conductors, most non-metallic materials such as air and plastics are good insulators – this is why electrical plugs have plastic covers and wires are encased in rubber.

In order for electrical current to flow there must be a closed path of a conductive material between two areas of different electrical charge. In most electrical circuits it is electrons flowing through metal wire that make up the electric current.

The strength of an electrical current is measured in amperes (amps) and depends on the resistance of the material the charge is flowing through (resistance is measured in ohms; conductors have lower resistance than insulators and so allow larger currents to flow) and the charge difference or electrical potential difference across the circuit. This potential difference is measured in volts and can be thought of as the force 'pushing' the electrical charges around the circuit.

Where does the name 'electricity' come from?

Both 'electricity' and 'electron' come from the Greek word for amber, which is electron.

Who was the first person to generate an electric current?

Michael Faraday, in 1831. He did this by moving a magnet in and out of a coil of wire, causing an electric current to travel through the wire.

Whenever electric current flows it generates heat in the material it flows through. The amount of heat depends on the strength of the current and the resistance of the material.

Power station to home: the electrical journey

In a power station (above), fuel is burned to heat water and turn it into steam. The steam pushes an enormous wheel, called a turbine, round at very high speeds. The turbine turns a huge dynamo called a generator, which makes electricity.

Putting the distribution lines for electricity underground protects not only the cables but also the beauty of the countryside.

Wind or water power can be used to turn a turbine and produce electricity. This cuts down on the use of fuels like coal and oil.

To get to the people who use it, the electricity first goes through a transformer which boosts its voltage so that it can be transferred more easily over long distances. It is then carried along power lines to substations near houses, factories and businesses. From the substation, it goes to all the places where it will be used. At the end of the electricity's journey, other transformers change it back into lower voltage electricity so it can be used safely.

Electricity entering your home passes through a meter, which records how much electricity you use. After that you can use it to switch on lights, kettles and computers. How many ways do you think we use electricity in our homes? Probably well over a hundred.

Lightning: electricity from the sky

In a storm cloud, moving air makes ice particles and water droplets rub together and become charged with static electricity. The positively charged particles then rise to the top of the cloud while the negatively charged ones sink to the bottom. The negative charges in the cloud are attracted to the ground – but because the air is an insulator the charges cannot flow. Instead the strength of the electric field between the cloud and the ground grows until it is strong enough to ionize the air, forming a conductive plasma. Once this happens the electric charges can flow from the cloud to the ground and the current that flows is so great that the air around it becomes white hot and explodes outwards, resulting in the bright flash of light and the sound of thunder. Benjamin Franklin, left (1706–90), an American scientist, conducted a dangerous experiment by flying a large kite up on a long string into a storm cloud. An iron key was tied to the end of the string, and the electrical charge from the cloud ran down the wet string and made sparks when it hit the key. Luckily, he was unhurt, and his discoveries led him to invent lightning conductors.

Wind farm

Energy natural *and* manufactured

Energy is what makes us grow and move. It is also heat, light, and sound. Plants store energy, and as they grow they obtain energy from the soil and light energy from the sun. This process is called photosynthesis.

Humans and animals get their energy from the nutrients and calories in food and drink. When you eat, your body uses food as fuel. Even when you think, you are using energy your body has gained from food you've eaten.

There are different kinds of energy. If you ride a bicycle, your body provides the energy to move the pedals and wheels. When a car moves, its energy comes from the fuel in its engine. We use energy to heat houses, power cars and buses, and for radios and factory machines. The technology we use in modern life requires a lot of energy.

Power station

Q&A?

What happens if a television is left on standby?

A television or stereo left on standby will use between 10% and 60% of the energy it would use if it were switched on.

How can I save energy?

Turn off lights when you leave a room, use energy-saving light bulbs, and never overfill the kettle.

A computer monitor left on overnight wastes the amount of energy it would take to print 800 pages.

fascinating **Facts**

Most of the power we use every day is from electrical energy. Electricity is very convenient as it can be easily carried by wires (above) to the electric sockets in our houses or stored in batteries. Most electricity is generated at power stations.

Power stations

Most power stations use fossil fuels such as coal, oil, and gas. The fuel is burned to heat water, which turns into steam, and the steam is used to move the parts of the generator, which produces electricity. Steam power was used to power trains in the early days of the railways.

Oil is also used to make the petrol that powers all our cars and buses. Fossil fuels are a finite resource: there is a limited supply of them, and we will eventually use them up. Many people ask what alternative energy sources we can use when the fossil fuels run out.

Hydroelectric power

Hydroelectric power is produced when the moving energy of falling water at river dams is used to power electric generators. The traditional version of this was the water wheel, used in small rivers and streams to power grain mills and early factories. Hydroelectric power can also be obtained from tidal energy using the twice-daily movement of the sea's tides.

Solar power

Solar power is produced when the energy from the sun is turned into electricity. Some people have solar panels (right) on the roofs of their houses to provide the power to heat the water for their baths or power their light bulbs. Solar

power plants are possible in very sunny parts of the world, but a wide area of ground would have to be covered by solar panels to provide sufficient electricity.

Wind power

Wind power is produced when turbines harness the power of the wind, especially in coastal areas where winds are strongest. Windmills have been used for hundreds of years as a source of power, but with modern technologies wind power can now be collected on a large scale from wind farms (below). Wind power is converted into electricity.

Nuclear power

Nuclear power is produced when a controlled nuclear reaction is used to power a large generator. Nuclear power stations create large amounts of energy, but the fuels they use are rare and expensive, and people worry that they are not safe and that they are harmful to the planet. There have been accidents at nuclear power stations in other countries, causing severe health problems from radioactivity. The waste from nuclear power stations is also radioactive and will remain so for thousands of years. So there is a problem of storing nuclear waste.

The European Union

The European Union (EU) is a group of democratic countries which have joined together. There are now 27 member states, and the EU has its own currency – the Euro. Not all of the countries use the Euro, preferring to keep their own currency.

Why a European Union?

Old frictions and rivalries between nations in the past led to instability or even war. Following World War I and World War II six European nations agreed to set up a group of countries within Europe who would work for permanent peace and also encourage trade between each other. They called themselves the European Economic Community (or the EEC or the Common Market). These first six countries were France, West Germany, Italy, Belgium, the Netherlands and Luxembourg. The name European Union came later because the purpose of the EEC changed from being simply a trading partnership into an economic and political partnership.

What has the EU achieved?

Since it was founded, the EU has:
- achieved over 50 years of peace in Europe
- helped to raise standards of living
- built a single Europe-wide market so that people, goods and money can move around as freely as if in one country
- launched the single EU currency, the Euro (€)
- strengthened Europe's position and voice in the world.

NORTH ATLANTIC OCEAN

Faeroe Is (Dmk)

North Sea

SWEDEN

DENMARK

REPUBLIC OF IRELAND

UNITED KINGDOM

NETHER-LANDS

GERMANY

POLAND

BELGIUM

LUX.

CZ.R.

SLA.

AUSTRIA

FRANCE

SL

HUNGARY

ROMAN

ITALY

BULG

PORTUGAL   SPAIN

GREECE

MALTA

Mediterranean S

EST

LATV

LITHUANIA

| 0 | 300 | 600 | 900 | 1200 miles |
| 0 | 500 | 1000 | 1500 | 2000 kilometres |

Which is the largest country in Europe?

By area France is the largest country, and Malta is the smallest. However, Germany has the largest population and again, Malta has the smallest.

Does the European Union have a president?

Yes. She or he is called the President of the Commission is selected by members of the European Council and is then approved by the European Parliament. The first president was Walter Hallstein from West Germany.

Euro notes are identical throughout the Euro area, while coins have a common design on one face and designs representing symbols unique to each country on the other face.

London, England, has the largest population of any city in the European Union, with over 7 million inhabitants. Berlin, in Germany, comes second with 3.5 million.

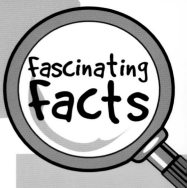

CZ.R.	CZECH REPUBLIC
LUX.	LUXEMBOURG
SLA.	SLOVAKIA
SL.	SLOVENIA

What if we didn't have the EU?

Try imagining a world now without the EU: we would still need to get our passports stamped when visiting nearby countries. We'd have to change our currency when we crossed from France to Spain. European businesses would be involved in constant negotiations when working with one another, without being able to look at agreed guidance and rules. Some of the poorer countries in Europe might not have benefited from trade partnerships and grants. And although counties might argue, we still have peace.

The European Parliament

A lot of people are needed to do all of the work that is carried out by the EU. The European Parliament represents around 450 million citizens. Its members are known as Members of the European Parliament (MEPs). Since the last European elections in 2004, there have been 732 MEPs.

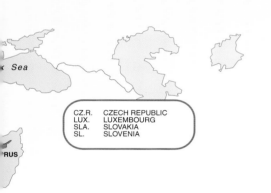

Where is the European Parliament?

The parliament meets in two places – in Brussels and in Strasbourg – and the European Court of Justice is in Luxembourg. The European Bank is in Frankfurt.
For three weeks of the month the parliament meets in Belgium's capital city Brussels, where most committee and political group meetings take place, then for one week everyone goes to Strasbourg in France. The Strasbourg Parliament on the border between Germany and France, which fought two world wars in the last century, is also a symbol of Europe's peaceful new order.

The current 27 member states:
Austria
Belgium
Bulgaria
Cyprus
Czech Republic
Denmark
Estonia
Finland
France
Germany
Greece
Hungary
Republic of Ireland
Italy
Latvia
Lithuania
Luxembourg
Malta
Poland
Portugal
Romania
Slovakia
Slovenia
Spain
Sweden
The Netherlands
United Kingdom

Explorers

Human beings have always been explorers. Ever since cavemen set out to discover what lay beyond the horizon, we have been fascinated by the unknown and the undiscovered.

The promise of adventure

Nowadays we have complicated and detailed maps of the world. We learn all about geography and the peoples of other lands in school, and we can go to zoos or read in books about animals like lions and elephants. But imagine setting sail across an ocean not knowing what you would find, or being the first person from your country ever to see an elephant! Exciting adventures like these, and the promise of great treasure, have led people to become explorers, despite knowing they would face terrible dangers.

Early European explorers

As people learned to read and write they began to leave records of their travels. The medieval explorer Marco Polo (1254–1324) was the first person to cross the whole of Asia and to leave journals of what he had seen. Many great European explorers followed his example, returning from their travels with new maps and new treasures, and astonishing tales of the strange animals and plants and ways of life they had discovered.

The age of discovery

The 15th and 16th centuries are known as the 'age of discovery'. At that time rival European countries, hungry for treasure and power, had powerful ships and navigational tools to help them sail the oceans in search of new lands. The Spanish king Charles I gave

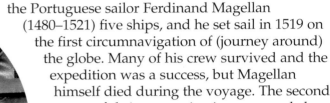

the Portuguese sailor Ferdinand Magellan (1480–1521) five ships, and he set sail in 1519 on the first circumnavigation of (journey around) the globe. Many of his crew survived and the expedition was a success, but Magellan himself died during the voyage. The second successful circumnavigation was made by an English privateer called Francis Drake (1542–1596). Drake was supported by Queen Elizabeth, who provided him with ships and supplies in return for a large share of the treasures he promised to find. Although Drake sailed around the world, the treasures with which he presented Elizabeth were actually stolen from Spanish galleons!

Treasures from the East

Many explorers did return with treasures, although not the gold and silver they dreamed of finding, but instead things like silks and spices from the Orient (right). Spices were at one time thought even more valuable than gold. They were highly prized by the wealthy for flavouring and preserving their food. For this reason we can see why the Portuguese explorer Vasco da Gama (1460–1524) became famous for discovering a new and fast trading route to India.

New territories

When explorers went looking for gold they found other treasures and sometimes discovered places by accident. This was not surprising, because they didn't have good maps and believed the earth was much smaller than it is. The most famous of all these accidents is the discovery of the Americas by Christopher Columbus. Columbus set sail in 1492 thinking that, because the world was round, sailing west would get him to the rich East more quickly and safely. Not knowing that America existed, he sailed right into it!

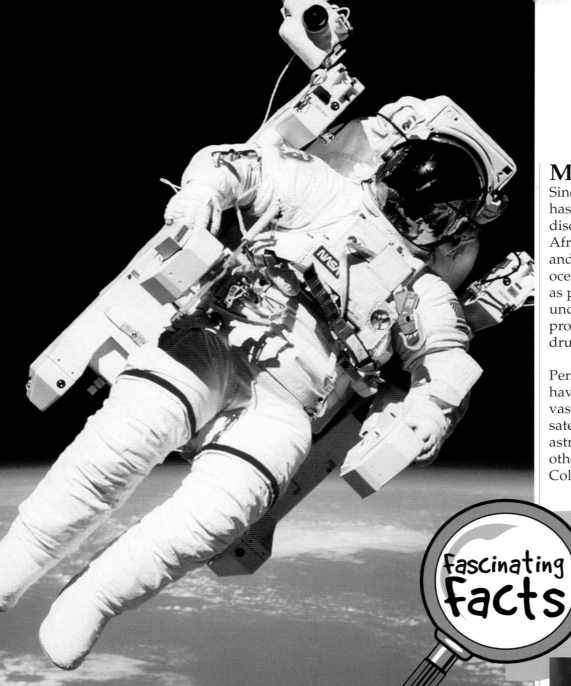

Modern explorers

Since the age of discovery, exploration has continued. Explorers have discovered tribes in the heart of African rainforests, reached the North and South Poles and explored deep oceans in submarines. Scientists such as plant hunters often search for undiscovered species that may provide the raw ingredients for new drugs to help cure disease.

Perhaps the most exciting place we have yet to explore fully is the vastness of space, into which we send satellites and probes. One day astronauts may set out to travel to other planets just as Magellan and Columbus travelled to other lands!

fascinating **facts**

Christopher Columbus sailed over 5,000 miles of open seas.

The plant hunters of previous centuries brought us many of the plants we see in our gardens today. For example, tulips originally grew only in Turkey (below).

Q&A?

Why do we sometimes refer to Native Americans as "Indians"?

That is what Christopher Columbus mistakenly called them, thinking he was in the East Indies!

What is Il Milione?

That is the original name of Marco Polo's book about his travels to China. The name comes from Polo's family nickname, Emilione. We usually call the book 'The Travels of Marco Polo'.

Fish *and* aquatic life

The world's oceans cover two-thirds of the Earth, and a huge variety of creatures live in the water. Fish constitute more than half the total number of known modern vertebrates (animals with backbones).

How do fish breathe?

Most fish breathe by using gills, which are made up of threadlike structures called filaments. Each filament has capillaries which give a large surface area for the exchange of oxygen and carbon dioxide. Fish take oxygen-rich water into their mouths, which is then pumped over the gills.

Fish need gills to breathe underwater

Crustaceans

There are approximately 39,000 species of crustaceans worldwide, including crabs, lobsters, shrimps, barnacles and woodlice. Most are aquatic (live in water) and the majority are marine (live in the sea).

Eels

Eels are fish that have evolved over time to lose their fins and scales. Some developed the ability to move over land, which is useful when they are stranded by receding floods. They are found in the sea and in fresh water. You may have seen puffins with lots of sand eels in their beaks.

Cnidaria

Cnidaria (with a silent c) are a group of animals including sea anemones, jellyfish and corals. Jellyfish are feared for their sting, which in some species can be deadly. The stings are caused by cells called nematocysts, which shoot out like miniature harpoons into their prey. The most dangerous species of jellyfish is the *Chironex fleckeri*, a box jellyfish from Australia. It is thought to have caused the death of more than 70 people during the 20th century in Australia alone!

Sea cucumbers

Despite their name, sea cucumbers are animals from the same family as sea urchins and starfish. In fact, they're more like giant leathery slugs than something to put in a salad. They come in all colours – from black to red-and-yellow-striped – and in all sizes. The largest is 2 m (6 ft) long.

Jellyfish

Puffin

Seahorses

The head of the seahorse resembles a horse's head, and its body has an elongated tail covered by about 50 rectangular bony plates (left). They can change colour so that they match their surroundings. This camouflage protects them from predators such as crabs, although with their bony armour there are very few animals that can eat them anyway. Seahorses are unique in that the male gives birth to the young and takes all responsibility for parental care.

What is a shark?

Unlike bony fish, sharks have no bones; their skeletons are made up of cartilage. Depending on their species sharks have five to seven pairs of gill openings (bony fish have one). The whale shark is the largest fish in the world.

It was probably named 'whale' because of its enormous size and the fact that, like most whales, it feeds by filtering water to take in small crustaceans and fish. However, cold-blooded and with gills, these huge animals are a species of shark and harmless to humans. The basking shark is the second largest fish. It can be found off the shores of Britain. But if you swim in the sea, don't worry, this gaping giant feeds on plankton!

Shark attack

Great whites are top of the list of man-eaters, and are responsible for five to ten attacks a year. Their powerful teeth are triangular and serrated, and a great white can have as many as 3,000! These fearsome predators hunt fish, sea lions, seals, turtles, porpoises, and other sharks. They usually attack from below, taking a large bite of their prey

Q&A?

How many types of fish are there?

Scientists have recognised an estimated 22,000 living species, and new species are being discovered all the time.

What are the largest and smallest fishes?

The largest is the whale shark, which is 16 m (51 ft). The smallest is a stout infantfish, which is 8 mm ($\frac{1}{4}$ in.) long.

and waiting for the victim to weaken from loss of blood. They can reach speeds of 40 km/h (25 mph) when in pursuit of prey, and have been known to leap out of the water. It is thought that shark attacks on humans are due to mistaken identity, as the silhouette of a swimmer viewed from below is similar to that of a seal or sea lion.

Sensory and nervous systems in fish

Most fishes possess highly developed sense organs. Nearly all daylight fish have well developed eyes with colour vision that is as least as good as human. Many fish also have an extraordinary sense of taste and smell. In 2003, scientists at Edinburgh University in Scotland found that fish experience pain when they performed experiments on rainbow trout.

Fascinating Facts

The electric eel isn't a true eel; it's actually the most powerful electric fish. It builds up electricity in specially modified muscles and gives off a shock that's enough to kill its prey. It can produce a lethal charge of up to 500 volts!

The yellow-bellied sea snake's venom is more poisonous than a cobra's. These snakes have been known to bite humans, but if treated with respect they are not usually aggressive.

Flight

Since the earliest days, people have looked up at the sky and imagined flying like birds. In the Greek legend, Icarus and his father made wings from feathers and wax, but Icarus flew too close to the sun, the wax melted, and he fell into the sea and drowned. In the real world, of course, they would not have been able to fly at all, because our arms are not strong enough for flight. In the natural world only birds, insects and some animals can fly. Birds use their wings to coast on warm, rising air currents. There are many different sizes and shapes of wings, and birds fly at different speeds.

people started to build machines to fly. They built gliders, which meant they could coast like birds on currents of air.

Balloon flight

The first recorded manned balloon flight in history was made in a hot air balloon built by the Montgolfier brothers on 21 November, 1783. The pilots, Jean-François Pilâtre de Rozier and Francois Laurent (the Marquis of d'Arlanders) flew for about 22 minutes.

Only a few days later Jacques Alexander Charles and Nicholas Louis Robert launched the first manned gas balloon. Again starting in Paris, the flight lasted over two hours and covered a distance of 56 km (25 miles).

Early attempts at flight

Inventors first attempted, around 400 BC, to copy the birds by making wings and strapping them to their arms. None of these attempts worked, however, so

When was the first commercial passenger service?

In 1914, between St Petersburg, Florida (USA) and Tampa, Florida (USA)

Who was the first woman to fly solo across the Atlantic?

Amelia Earhart (1897–1937) made a transatlantic solo flight in 1932.

Ballooning became fashionable and popular in the 18th century, and Ferdinand von Zeppelin made the first flight in a zeppelin (a type of airship) in 1900.

Aircraft

Aircraft are heavier than air but use thrust (forward motion created by the engine) to stay aloft. It was not until the start of the 20th century that heavier-than-air machines achieved flight. In 1903, the Wright brothers (Wilbur and Orville) built the first manned, power-driven, heavier-than-air flying machine. Their first flight was only 12 seconds long.

Acrobatic flying became popular, and newspapers offered large cash prizes for daredevil stunts. Long-distance flying also developed and an English newspaper sponsored a contest for the first flight across the English Channel. Louis Bleriot won this contest, flying from France to England in 1909 in a single wing plane. The first woman to gain a pilot's licence was Baroness Raymonde de la Roche (1884–1919), and the first aircraft to take off from water was flown by Henri Fabre (1882–1984).

Aircraft in wartime

The First World War was instrumental in the development of planes, from experiments to fully working machines. It was soon discovered that, to win the war, air control was vital. Aerial information, bombing and support provided valuable support to ground troops. World War I saw the birth of the fighter aircraft, or 'scouts', which still play a crucial role in modern history. The war also advanced bomber planes, so that they went from carrying only small bombs to deadly cargoes on purpose-built racks and housing.

In the 1930s both military and civil aircraft underwent a period of

development. Commercial air travel was an accepted form of transport. The first airliners were born, and they began crossing larger distances. More and more record-breaking flights were also being achieved. In 1927 Charles Lindbergh flew the first solo non-stop flight across the North Atlantic in his Ryan NYP monoplane, *Spirit of St Louis*.

Concorde

The Anglo-French machine Concorde was one of the world's greatest challenges in the history of aviation (flying). It cruised at more than twice the speed of sound at an altitude of 20,000 m (60,000 ft – eleven miles high). A typical flight from London to New York took fewer than four hours. Production of the plane ended in 1979, and all Concordes were withdrawn from service in 2000 after a crash near the Charles de Gaulle airport, Paris.

Helicopters

Helicopters were developed in the 20th century. The early designs were very unsuccessful, although some designs go back as far as the Renaissance artist and inventor Leonardo da Vinci's sketchbooks. Helicopters are used in war, to transport troops quickly, evacuate injured soldiers, and also to fight. In the civilian world, helicopters can be used as 'air ambulances' to reach injured people quickly, and get them to hospital.

Helicopters can land in quite remote and restricted places as they don't need a runway for landing or taking off as most aeroplanes do.

Fascinating Facts

Hans-Ulrich Rudel of Germany flew 2,530 combat missions during World War Two, and survived.

Human-powered and solar-powered aircraft have made successful flights across the English Channel.

Food *and* healthy eating

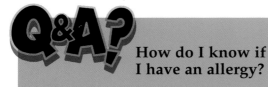

Healthy eating means having a healthy, balanced diet. Eating a range of foods every day is just as important to maintaining good health as taking regular exercise. Nutritional needs vary according to an individual's age and lifestyle. Eating too many foods which are not good for us can lead to being overweight and can also cause illness.

What is a balanced diet?

Generally having a good balance of grain foods, vegetables, fresh fruit, meat or fish and dairy products is considered to be healthy. It's better for our health if we don't eat too many sugary or fatty foods such as sweets and chips. Vegetarians, people who don't eat meat, should take care that they get enough protein from their food by eating nuts or pulses (peas and beans). The elements essential to a balanced diet are:

- Grain foods: bread, rice, cereals and pasta – 6–11 servings each day.
- Vegetables: especially green leafy vegetables like broccoli – 3–5 servings each day.

- Fresh fruit: 2–4 servings each day.
- Protein such as meat, fish, eggs, nuts, beans: 2–3 servings each day.
- Dairy products such as cheese and yogurt: 2-3 servings every other day.

What's wrong with fast food?

Fast foods like burgers and deep fried foods are often very high in calories (units of energy) but low in nutrients. This means that it is very easy to gain weight by eating these foods, unless we take a great deal of exercise, but we also need other foods to provide essential nutrients.

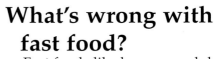

Q&A?

| How do I know if I have an allergy? | *People with allergies may suffer from skin rashes, sickness or breathing difficulties if they eat the wrong food.* |
| Why should I exercise? | *Exercise, as well as eating sensible food, helps to keep our body healthy and active.* |

Sugar on our teeth turns into acid within five minutes! The acid begins to dissolve the tooth surface and very soon dental decay occurs.

Did you know that more than half of your weight is just water? So as well as giving your body all the food it needs each day to keep healthy, you need at least five glasses of liquid each day.

What about salt and sugar?

Salt helps to flavour food and to keep it fresh longer, but can lead to health problems such as high blood pressure if we have too much. Sugar is found naturally in fruit but high consumption of processed sugar, which is made from sugar cane or sugar beet, can lead to weight problems and to diabetes. Because salt and sugar are contained in many ready-made foods which we buy it is often difficult to know how much we are consuming so adding as little as possible to foods is a good way to keep our consumption down.

What are allergies?

Some people are allergic to certain foods or ingredients. If you have an allergy it is important to check your food otherwise you may become ill. Some common allergies, which many people suffer from, are peanuts, shellfish, artificial dyes and colours. The labels on foods we buy usually have detailed nutritional information to help us to avoid foods which may make us ill.

Why is exercise important?

Exercise is important for many reasons – the best being because it keeps your body healthy. Daily exercise helps prevent diseases, improves stamina, controls weight and will improve your quality of life. Like food, exercise should be balanced – building up a daily routine that mirrors the lifestyle that you lead.

Genetics

Genetics is the study of heredity, evolution and all life forms. Every human has similar characteristics, such as hair, legs and eyes, and genes are the instructions which make us all different, giving us blue or brown eyes, red or black hair. Genes are like the instructions that govern how every living creature looks and functions. The genetic information that makes us individual is inherited through chromosomes from our parents.

Each paired chromosome is composed of two tightly coiled strands of DNA (Deoxyribonucleic acid) that join in the middle to form an X shape. These strands of DNA have sections called genes, which contain the information that makes us unique. Unless you have an identical twin, your DNA is different from the DNA of every other person in the world, though it is the same in every cell in your body,

The vast majority of people have two copies of each gene, as we get one copy from each of our parents.

There is one copy of each gene on one of the pair of chromosomes we receive from our parents. As we receive two sets of instructions, this could cause confusion. But usually one gene is dominant: for example the gene for brown eyes is dominant over the gene for blue eyes (the gene for blue eyes is said to be recessive). In order to inherit blue eyes, a child must inherit two copies of the eye gene for blue eyes, one from each parent.

A momentous discovery

In 1953 two scientists, James D. Watson and Francis Crick, celebrated the fact that they had unravelled the structure of DNA. DNA is the material that makes up genes which pass hereditary characteristics from one parent to another. That momentous discovery was the culmination of research by scientists Maurice Wilkins and Rosalind Franklin. Powerful and controversial technologies are now available, including genetic engineering, stem cell research and DNA fingerprinting.

DNA fingerprinting

Each person's DNA is as unique as a fingerprint. Normal fingerprints occur only on the fingertips and can be altered by surgery. DNA 'fingerprints', however, can be taken even from bloodstained clothing and cannot be altered by any known treatment. Everyone has a different sequence of DNA. By identifying repeated patterns of DNA, scientists can identify whether DNA samples are from the same person, related people or people who are not related.

Can we clone dinosaurs?

We have only found a small proportion of the genetic information for dinosaurs so far. It is therefore not possible to clone a dinosaur at the moment, but it may be possible in the future.

What is DNA fingerprinting used for?

DNA fingerprinting can be used for anything from determining a biological mother or father to identifying the suspect of a crime.

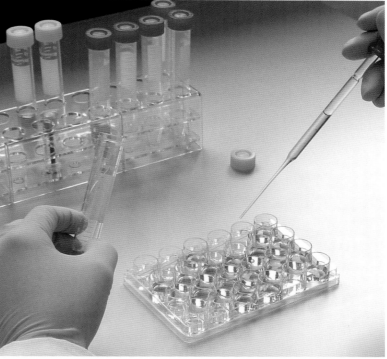

Stem cell research

Stem cells are cells that are present in the very early stages of an embryo's development. They can develop into any type of specialised cell. Stem cell research is investigating ways to produce cells to replace those damaged by diseases, such as Parkinson's Disease.

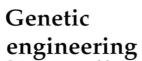

Genetic engineering

Scientists are able to manipulate genes using genetic engineering. For years humans have been breeding animals and plants to get the characteristics they desire, for example, species that produce a lot of babies or new plants. Two techniques used to do this are selective breeding (breeding animals and plants by controlling the environment) and cross breeding (breeding species with the same ancestors). A clone is any organism whose genetic information is identical to that of a 'mother organism' from which it was created. Some clones exist in nature; others are created by scientists. Dolly the sheep was the first mammal cloned from an adult cell.

Fascinating Facts

James Watson, Francis Crick and Maurice Wilkins were awarded the Nobel Prize for their work in 1962. Rosalind Franklin died of cancer in April 1958, aged just 37, so never received a Nobel Prize for her crucial work in the discovery of DNA.

A giant model of a section of DNA, built from laboratory clamps and pieces of metal, is now in the Science Museum in London.

Global warming

Many scientists believe that gases in the air are causing the Earth's climate to gradually become hotter. This is called global warming.

Temperature and climate change

Measurements from the past 100 years show that the Earth's temperature has increased by 0.6°C (1°F). But scientists expect that over the next 100 years it will increase by an extra 1–3°C (2–6°F). This may not sound like much, but it could make the difference between life and death for some species on Earth, and dramatic changes to our climate!

What is the greenhouse effect?

In the Earth's atmosphere are tiny amounts of gases called 'greenhouse gases'. These gases let the sun's rays pass through to the Earth but hold in the heat that comes up from the sun-warmed Earth. This is called the 'greenhouse effect' – a natural process by which the Earth's atmosphere traps some of the sun's energy. It is this warmth that allows the Earth to support life – just as a greenhouse in your garden traps heat to keep growing plants warm enough.

A natural process gone wrong

Most scientists believe humans are now creating too many greenhouse gases, unnaturally increasing the greenhouse effect. When too many greenhouse gases are added to the atmosphere, the 'walls' of our greenhouse (the 'thermal blanket') get thicker. More heat gets trapped in the atmosphere and the temperature of the Earth goes up. A process that has been beneficial to life on Earth becomes potentially harmful.

What is causing global warming?

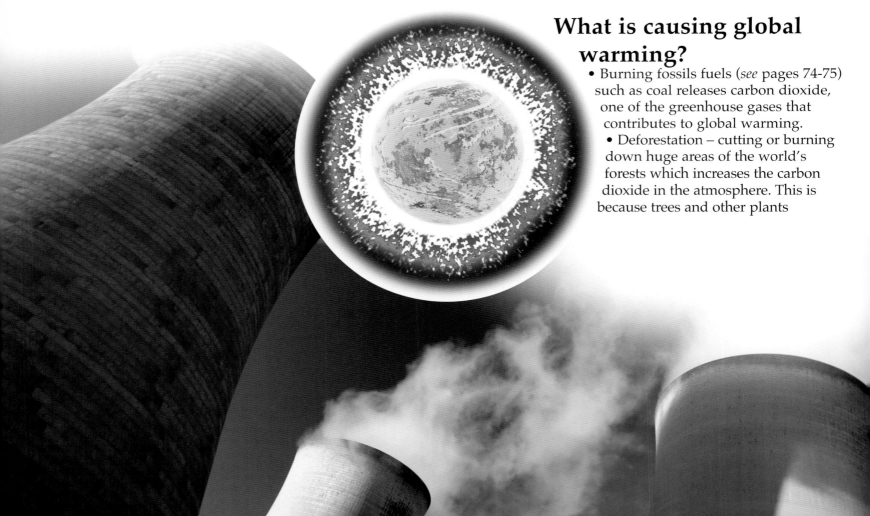

- Burning fossils fuels (*see* pages 74-75) such as coal releases carbon dioxide, one of the greenhouse gases that contributes to global warming.
- Deforestation – cutting or burning down huge areas of the world's forests which increases the carbon dioxide in the atmosphere. This is because trees and other plants

The last Ice Age was a mere 7°F colder than today. That's a little less than 4°C!

The six hottest recorded years in history were all in the 1990s.

'breathe in' carbon dioxide and 'breathe out' oxygen, thus helping to lower the amounts of carbon dioxide in our air.

• As rubbish decays, another harmful greenhouse gas called methane is released into the atmosphere.

Q&A?

How long have we known about the greenhouse effect?

The French scientist Joseph Fourier first wrote about this in 1824, though he didn't call it the greenhouse effect.

Possible consequences of global warming

Melting ice Ice covers 3% of the Earth's surface and is the world's largest supply of fresh water. Warmer weather causes glaciers (huge, slow-moving sheets of ice) – and even the polar ice caps – to melt. Many of our glaciers are already melting.

Rising seas Melting glaciers add water to the ocean. Rising sea levels would mean coastal flooding and could cause salt water to flow into areas where salt would harm plants and animals.

Droughts and diseases Cold places on the Earth may become warmer, and this could mean a chance to plant crops in places that were formerly too cold.

However, areas that already have hot climates might become too hot, bringing drought and leaving people without enough to eat. Tropical diseases like malaria might become more common in newly warmed areas.

Extreme weather A warmer world is expected to experience more extreme weather – more rain during wet times, more powerful storms and longer periods of drought.

What can we do?

There are many things people can do to help stop global warming. These are just some of them:

• *Save electricity* Use low-energy light bulbs and switch things off when they are not needed.
• *Reduce car use* Walk, cycle or take the bus.

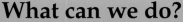

• *Recycle* Plastic bags, cans, newspapers and many other items can be recycled, so that less rubbish goes to landfill sites. Buy recyclable products instead of non-recyclable ones.
• *Reuse* Even better than recycling is using things again. Buy things that have less packaging and create less waste.
• *Choose items carefully* Some cars are better for the environment than others because they can travel longer on a smaller amount of fuel.
• *Plant trees* Trees absorb carbon dioxide from the air.

Gravity

Force is the pressure used when something is pushed or pulled. Forces are all round us. When you throw a ball in the air, it is pulled back to the ground by gravity. Gravity is a natural force that pulls objects on or near the Earth's surface towards its centre. In other words, it keeps us all fixed to the surface of the earth.

Gravity keeps the moon going round the Earth, the Earth going round the sun, and the sun going round the centre of the Milky Way. It's the force that governs motion in the universe.

Objects with mass (a measure of weight) attract each other, no matter how small or large they are. The strength of attraction depends on the weight of the objects and the distance between them.

In orbit

An object remains in orbit around a mass, such as a planet, due to that planet's gravity. For instance, the Earth is surrounded by it's own gravitational field, and so objects in orbit around the Earth are attracted to the Earth and therefore maintain their orbit.

Are clouds affected by gravity?

No, because clouds are made of very small particles of ice and water and are too light, and so they just float. However, they can combine together and form rain drops The rain drops are much bigger and so gravity pulls them down.

Is gravity the same everywhere?

Gravity at the equator is slightly less than at the North Pole, because the Earth bulges at the equator and you are further from the centre of the Earth.

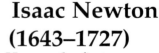

Isaac Newton (1643–1727)

He was the first person to study gravity seriously, and he had the insight to realise that the force that holds us to the Earth is the same one that keeps the planets in their orbits around the sun. He worked out the mathematical nature of the mutual (two-way) force, and he correctly argued that gravity acts across the entire universe.

Kepler wrote science fiction stories.

Astronauts discovered many changes in their bodies by living in a 'weightless' environment. Their bones lost calcium, their kidneys worked harder, there was excess fluid in their faces and chests, their muscles and hearts shrank.

Newton had read Galileo and Johannes Kepler's work on how planets circle the sun and how things fall to the Earth. Galileo (1564–1642) was an Italian physicist, astronomer and philosopher. Kepler (1571–1630) was a German mathematician, astronomer and astrologer. He wondered whether the force that kept the moon from being thrown away from the Earth could explain gravity on the Earth's surface. Newton made this link in 1666, and called his findings the Law of Universal Gravitation. There is a famous story that Newton made the connection between the two ideas because of an apple falling in an orchard. However, it is more likely that the idea did not come to him in a flash of inspiration, but was developed over time.

Albert Einstein

Newton's description remained unchanged until Albert Einstein published his General Theory of Relativity in 1915. Einstein modified Newton's view of gravity by arguing that the gravitational force is a sign of the curvature of space-time. Although Einstein's idea is necessary for describing the evolution of the universe as a whole, Newton's theory works well enough when gravitational forces are not very strong.

The Greeks

In the period before the Roman empire, from about 776 BC to the death of Alexander in 323 BC, ancient Greece was the most important civilisation in western Europe. The ancient Greeks lived in a society that valued individual freedom within the law, and promoted excellence in sport, learning and the arts. Greek civilisation has left us many legacies, including many of the words we use today and the Olympic Games.

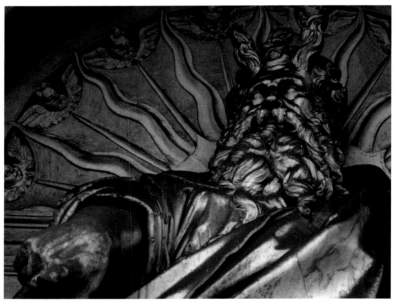

Ancient Greece was not a single nation, but made up of a number of city-states called polis which were dotted across the mainland, the islands of the Aegean and Ionian seas, and along the coast of what is now Turkey.

Athens, named after Athena, the goddess of wisdom and the city's patron, was the intellectual centre of Greece, and one of the first city-states.

Culture

The artistic talents of the Athenians can be viewed through many different forms which have survived for centuries, such as architectural designs, sculptures, pottery and fine jewellery.

At the Theatre of Dionysia, named after the god of wine, a religious festival was held in honour of the gods. For ten days Athenians filled the theatre to see plays performed by their favourite poets and playwrights. Women were not allowed to take part. The men wore elaborate masks and costumes while performing both male and female roles.

The Olympics

The Olympic Games were the greatest national festival for the Athenians. Held every four years, athletes came from all regions of Greece to compete in the great Stadium of Olympia and honour their supreme god, Zeus. At the conclusion of the games, the winners were presented with garlands and crowned with olive wreaths.

Life in ancient Greece

Athenian soldiers were required to serve two years in the military. After the first year, they were given a sword and a shield with the state's emblem on it. Although they served only two years, they could be called at any moment up to the age of sixty. Most wars between city-states were due to problems concerning harvests or livestock, and lasted only a day or so. Heralds were government officials who travelled throughout Greece carrying important messages for their city-states. They held a special stick as a sign of their authority and were under the protection of the messenger god Hermes – people were not allowed to attack them, even during war, as this was seen as breaking international law. Farmers kept goats, sheep, pigs and chickens. Crops were grains, grapes and olives. Gods were usually served by priests in

Why did the actors play male and female roles?

Women were not allowed to participate in dramatic activities.

What was the most important event at the Olympic Games?

The pentathlon, where an athlete competed in five different events.

ancient Greece, and goddesses were served by priestesses. Often the job was for life, but some priests and priestesses were

ordinary citizens who served for two to four years, or just during religious festivals. Their duties ranged from supervising rituals and taking part in festivals, to conducting weddings and funerals.

Mythology

The Gods were described as having essentially human, but ideal bodies.

Zeus was the chief god. The gods and goddesses were said to live on Mount Olympia. Each god or goddess had a particular area of interest. For example, Poseidon was god of the sea, Persephone goddess of the seasons, Apollo drove his chariot across the sky for the sun. Greek gods were said to have many fantastic abilities, such as being able to disguise themselves, transport themselves to any location, are not affected by disease, can be wounded only under highly unusual circumstances, and they are immortal.

This is a collection of stories that explain how the world began and described the lives of the gods and goddesses as well as of the ordinary people. The stories are passed down to us through oral and written traditions as well as from vase paintings.

The Cyclops were giants who were thrown into the underworld by their brother Cronus. But Zeus, son of Cronus, released the giants and in gratitude they gave him the gifts of thunder and lightning. So he became ruler of the Olympian gods.

Letters from the Greek alphabet are still used today, especially in science. Examples are α, β, γ, μ, θ, π and Ω. For example, the formula for finding the area of a circle $c = \pi \times radius^2$.

Fascinating facts

The human body *and* health

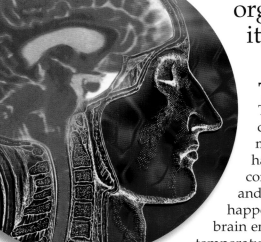

The human body is made up of bones, muscles, internal organs and skin. The bones act like a frame. Muscles are attached to bones and make it possible to move. Internal organs are responsible for the functions that keep us alive. The brain controls these and, together with the central nervous system allows us to be aware of what is happening around us. Skin is an organ that covers the whole of the body, protecting it, and preventing it from drying out.

The brain

The brain works like a central computer monitoring what is happening outside and continually monitoring and adjusting what is happening inside. The brain ensures that body temperature is kept constant and that there is enough oxygen and glucose in the blood.

The digestive and respiratory systems

All parts of the body need a mixture of oxygen and glucose (energy). The digestive and respiratory systems provide these. The digestive system is made up of the mouth, the gullet, the stomach, and the small and large intestines. Food taken in through the mouth is broken down and the energy that it contains is absorbed. The waste products remaining eventually form faeces in the bowel. The respiratory system is made up of the nose and lungs. As we breathe oxygen is taken in and carbon dioxide is exhaled.

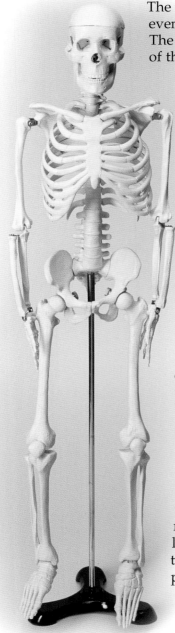

Oxygen and energy

Oxygen and energy are moved round the body by the circulatory system, which is made up of the heart and blood vessels. Blood is kept flowing through the circulatory system by the pumping action of the heart. Oxygen and energy are taken to muscles and carbon dioxide and other waste products are carried away. Carbon dioxide is taken to the lungs where it is breathed out. Other waste products are taken to the liver and kidneys. These organs filter the blood, removing waste products. Waste products removed by the kidneys go into the urine and some of those removed by the liver go into the large intestine. Urine collects in the bladder, which is emptied periodically.

What is the largest organ in the body?

The skin.

How many times will the human heart beat in an average lifetime?

Your heart beats about 100,000 times in one day and about 35,000,000 times in a year. That's 2,800,000,000 times in an average lifetime!

Every 30 days we have a completely new skin.

There are more than 200 different bones in the human body.

The small intestine is 5 metres long.

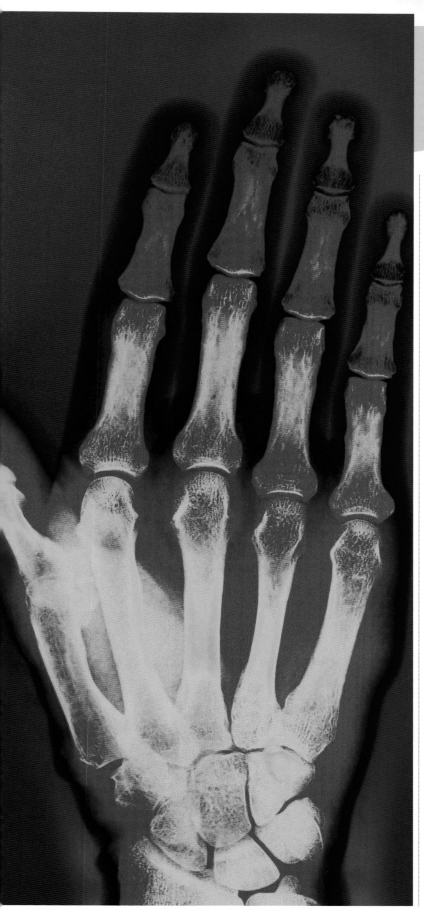

The senses

The senses are the way in which we know about the world around us – they are sight, hearing, smell, taste and touch.

Eyes are designed much like a camera. Light enters through the pupil, and is focused by the lens on the retina – the light-sensitive surface at the back of the eye. This information goes to the brain.

There are two parts to the ear: the outer ear (the part we can see) and the ear canal – a tube that goes into the head. In the middle ear is the eardrum. Sound waves make the eardrum vibrate and the vibrations are passed along three tiny bones to the inner ear (cochlea) which converts the movements into information that the brain interprets as sound.

The sense of smell depends on a collection of cells at the back of the nose, that are sensitive to minute quantities of chemicals, for example those given off by freshly baked bread.

The 'taste' of something is really a combination of smell and taste. When we eat or drink the tongue detects the basic tastes – sweet, sour, bitter and salty, and we also smell it. The brain puts both together and comes up with the overall taste.

Touch is different from the other senses because we have a sense of touch all over the body. Nerve endings in the skin can detect cold, heat, pain and pressure. Together these make up the sense of touch.

Keeping the body healthy

Keeping the body healthy involves:
- Eating a balanced diet to ensure that you have enough energy for activity and enough nutrients to grow and repair.
- Taking regular exercise to keep the muscles strong and the lungs clear.
- Getting enough sleep.
- Not smoking cigarettes because they contain chemicals that do long term damage to the lungs, heart and blood vessels.

Insects

Insects make up the largest group of animals on the planet. They first appeared on the Earth more than 500 million years ago and exist in almost every part of the world. There are at least a million species of insect ranging from ants, beetles and butterflies to bees and wasps. They can vary in size, from the very smallest which are almost invisible to humans, to some very large beetles.

Development

Most insects hatch from eggs, and all go through different stages of development to become adults. In some species an egg hatches to become a larva, which is something like a worm. The larva grows and becomes a pupa, sometimes sealed up in a cocoon or chrysalis. After further changes, the adult emerges. The butterfly is one insect that follows this type of development.

How do insects affect human life?

Some insects are considered pests, for example termites, lice and flies. Some are merely nuisances, although others can cause many problems by spreading disease to crops and humans. Many insects, however, are very beneficial to both people and the environment. Some insects are very important because they pollinate flowers to produce seed and fruit. We have always relied on honeybees for honey, and the silk produced by silkworms played an important role in opening up trade with China many years ago.

What is the most dangerous insect?

The mosquito is probably the most dangerous insect because it carries deadly diseases such as malaria.

How many species of insect are there?

There are probably at least a million different species of insect ranging from ants and butterflies, to bees and wasps. Not all species have been identified, so there could be as many as 30 million!

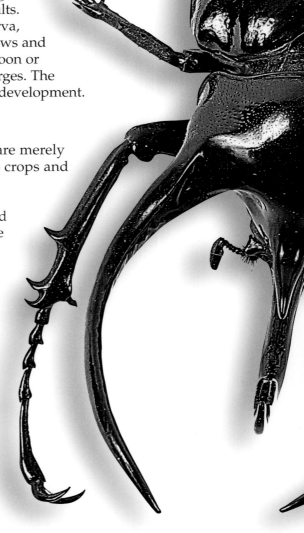

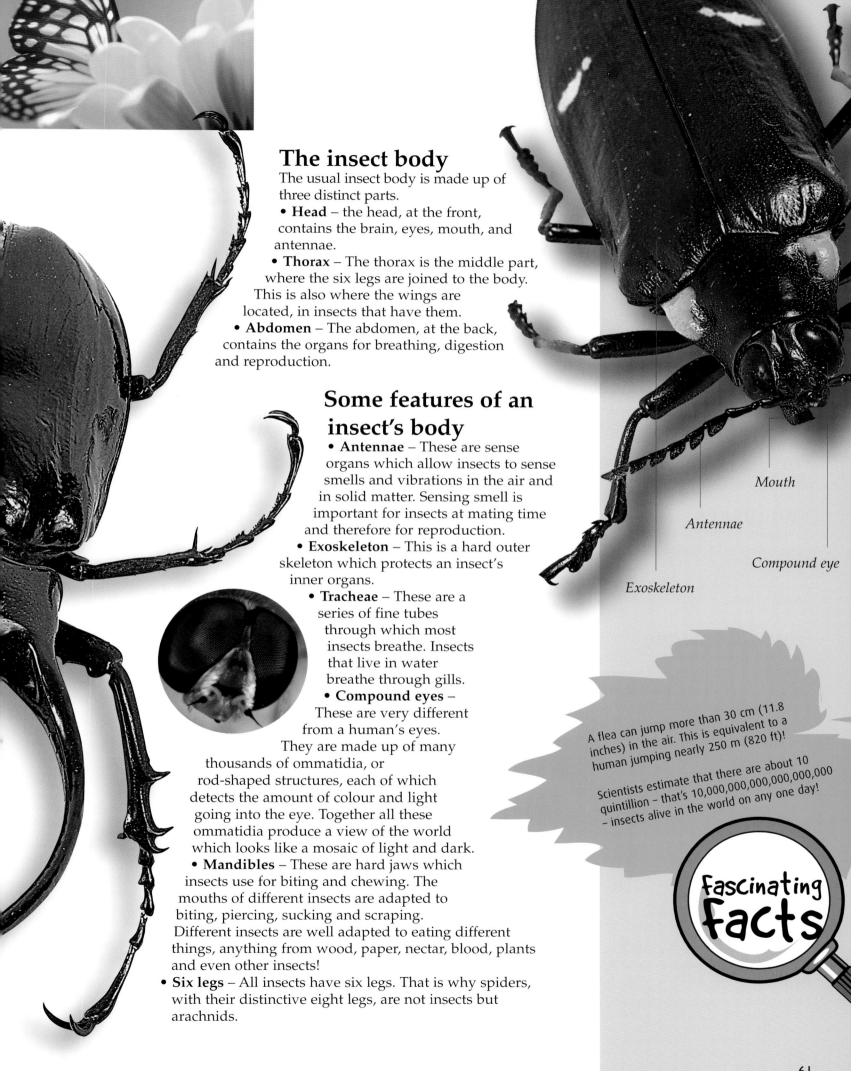

The insect body

The usual insect body is made up of three distinct parts.

• **Head** – the head, at the front, contains the brain, eyes, mouth, and antennae.

• **Thorax** – The thorax is the middle part, where the six legs are joined to the body. This is also where the wings are located, in insects that have them.

• **Abdomen** – The abdomen, at the back, contains the organs for breathing, digestion and reproduction.

Some features of an insect's body

• **Antennae** – These are sense organs which allow insects to sense smells and vibrations in the air and in solid matter. Sensing smell is important for insects at mating time and therefore for reproduction.

• **Exoskeleton** – This is a hard outer skeleton which protects an insect's inner organs.

• **Tracheae** – These are a series of fine tubes through which most insects breathe. Insects that live in water breathe through gills.

• **Compound eyes** – These are very different from a human's eyes. They are made up of many thousands of ommatidia, or rod-shaped structures, each of which detects the amount of colour and light going into the eye. Together all these ommatidia produce a view of the world which looks like a mosaic of light and dark.

• **Mandibles** – These are hard jaws which insects use for biting and chewing. The mouths of different insects are adapted to biting, piercing, sucking and scraping. Different insects are well adapted to eating different things, anything from wood, paper, nectar, blood, plants and even other insects!

• **Six legs** – All insects have six legs. That is why spiders, with their distinctive eight legs, are not insects but arachnids.

Mouth

Antennae

Compound eye

Exoskeleton

A flea can jump more than 30 cm (11.8 inches) in the air. This is equivalent to a human jumping nearly 250 m (820 ft)!

Scientists estimate that there are about 10 quintillion – that's 10,000,000,000,000,000,000 – insects alive in the world on any one day!

fascinating Facts

Language *and* communication

Communication means passing on information from one person to another, or to many people at the same time. When we say or write something to another person, or even just wave at them to say 'hello', we are communicating with them.

We do not have to use words to communicate – we can use other methods:
- Sound – like a fire-engine siren or a school bell.
- Signs – road signs can tell us how fast we are allowed to drive.
- Lights – an ambulance's flashing blue light means 'Get out of the way!'

Languages
To understand what someone else is saying to us, we need to know the same language as they do. Some languages are spoken by millions of people, others by less than a dozen.

Sign languages
Deaf people use 'manual language', making signs with their hands and fingers. A system of raised dots called Braille allows blind people to read by running their fingers over a page. You will also see bumps on pavements which warn blind people when they are approaching a hazard.

If you have ever used smileys in your text messages or emails, you have used sign language.

The spoken word
Spoken language was around for centuries before writing came into use. Memorising words was the only way to record anything. Many early societies did not write down their histories and tales, but people learned them by heart, and passed them on using speech. We call this oral history. Oral means 'by mouth' or 'spoken'.

The written word
People are believed to have started using writing around 6,000 BC. Ancient writing used pictures to represent words.

About 3,500 years ago, writing underwent its most important change. A people called the Phoenicians developed an alphabet. In an alphabet, symbols represent sounds rather than ideas or pictures.

Combinations of these 'sound letters' can be used to make up words in more than one language.

The picture language of the Ancient Egyptians was called hieroglyphic.

The most common alphabet we use in the West today is called the Roman alphabet.

The printed word
The first books were hand-written, and very few people could read them. This all changed in the West with the development of the printing press by Johann Gutenberg in 1450. Large numbers of books could now be printed quickly and cheaply. A statue (above right) to commemorate his contribution to printing can be seen in Mainz, Germany, which is where Gutenberg came from.

In 1803 the first paper-making machine was invented, and in 1810 a printing press was first driven by steam power.

Fascinating **Facts**

Books do not have to be words printed on paper: we can now listen to books recorded on audio tapes and CDs, and we can download books from the Internet to read on our computer screens.

The transmitted word – and moving pictures

In 1844, the building of the first telegraph system enabled near-instant written communication over distance.

In 1876, the telephone was invented. Alexander Graham Bell (1847–1922), a Scottish scientist and inventor, is widely considered as one of the developers of the telephone. In 1877, sound was first recorded. People could listen to music played on phonographs (early sound systems) in their homes. In 1895, the first radio message was sent.

In the 1830s, photography allowed images to be captured, and in the 1890s moving pictures (the movies) arrived. One of the most familiar objects in our homes today is the television. John Logie Baird (1888–1946), a Scottish engineer, is best known as the inventor of the first working electromechanical television system. This became popular in the late 1940s.

In 1962, the first communications satellite was launched into space. It made the first ever 'live' television broadcast to the United States, Europe, Japan and South America.

World Wide Web

The Internet, or World Wide Web, was developed in the late 1960s, and is now a popular way to communicate and find information.

Data (information) can be transmitted between computers. This allows people to send each other messages via email (electronic mail), or 'chat' by typing on-screen.

 **What do we call a person who is unable to speak?**

The medical term is aphonia, and we would say that a person is aphonic. But these aren't commonly used words. Today we would say that a person 'lacked the power of speech', or that they were 'voiceless'.

What is the most common sentence that is used to test typewriters and computer keyboards

'The quick brown fox jumps over the lazy dog'. This sentence contains all of the letters of the alphabet. It is called a pangram. There are other pangrams but this is the shortest and most memorable.

Sun and wind

Sunlight, or solar energy, can be used directly for heating and lighting homes and offices, for generating electricity, and for heating water. Solar power can also be used in factories.

Hydropower

Falling water can be used to drive a turbine – a spinning machine which makes electricity. This is called hydropower (hydro and water). Waterfalls can be used to make hydropower. Sometimes an existing waterfall is used, or a dam can be built on a river to make a new waterfall.

Biomass

The living material in plants is called biomass. Biomass can be used to produce electricity, chemicals or fuel for cars. For example, the oil in some plants can be used to make a kind of petrol.

How can waves be used to make electricity?

The tides and the winds drive the waves. The oceans move forward and back, following a regular pattern. The energy of the tides can be captured by special machines.

What is geothermal energy?

The inside of the Earth is very hot. Geothermal energy uses the Earth's internal heat for various uses. This energy from the Earth can be used to heat buildings or make electricity.

fascinating Facts

The average household throws away almost 8.5 kg (19 lb) of paper each week. Most types of paper can be recycled; the more paper we recycle the fewer trees need to be cut down – because paper is made from pulped trees!

Hydrogen is the most abundant element on the Earth. It can be burned as a fuel, or converted into electricity.

New Zealand

New Zealand lies halfway between the Equator and the South Pole. It is over 1,931 km (1,200 miles) from Australia and comprises two main islands plus smaller ones. The South Island is the largest land mass, and is divided along its length by the Southern Alps, the highest peak of which is Aoraki/Mount Cook, 3,754 m (12,316 ft) high. There are 18 peaks of more than 3,000 m (9,800 ft) in the South Island. The tallest mountain on North Island is Mount Ruapehu, an active cone volcano, 2,797 m (9,176 ft) high.

The Maori

The Maori were the first settlers. They arrived from Polynesia some time after the 13th century and established their own culture. New Zealand's Maori name is Aotearoa, and is usually translated as 'Land of the long white cloud', supposedly referring to the cloud the explorers saw on the horizon as they approached.

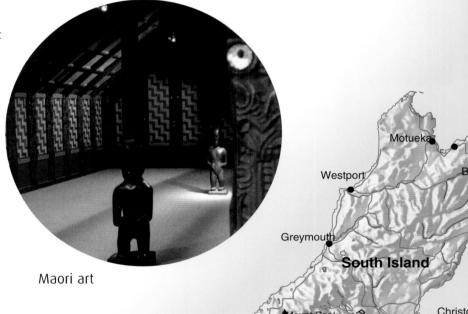

Maori art

Why are New Zealanders called Kiwis?

The kiwi, a small flightless bird only found in New Zealand, has become the country's national symbol.

What is New Zealand's main team sport?

Rugby. New Zealand's international team is known as the 'All Blacks' due to their black shirts and shorts.

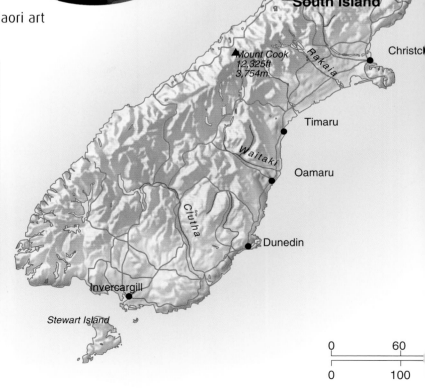

New Ply

Motueka

Westport

Bl

Greymouth

South Island

Christc

Mount Cook
12,325ft
3,754m

Rakaia

Timaru

Waitaki

Oamaru

Clutha

Dunedin

Invercargill

Stewart Island

| 0 | 60 |
| 0 | 100 |

The Waimangu Geyser is the largest ever known. Scalding water is thrown up to 450 m (1,476 ft) into the air. In 1903 four people were killed when they were thrown 800 m (2,625 ft) by one eruption.

The four stars on the New Zealand flag stand for the Southern Cross constellation of stars as seen in the sky from New Zealand.

The Maori lived in fortified villages. The wood carvings used to decorate the buildings is their main art style. Over 1,000 Maori meeting houses with intricately carved designs are still in existence.

Colonial settlers

The first Europeans known to have reached New Zealand arrived in 1642. They developed commercial farming and the country's industrial base. Most people live in the cities of the warmer, volcanic North Island, where Auckland is the largest city and Wellington is the capital.

Flora and fauna

New Zealand is very isolated from other countries and therefore around 80% of the plants and trees are found only in New Zealand, such as the giant kauri and southern beech.

Before the arrival of humans during the 1300s there were no land mammals in New Zealand. Birds, bats and sea creatures, some of which are now extinct, were the only animals to be found. It is still the case that some of the animals are found only on these islands. The weta is one such insect. There are about 70 varieties of weta; the largest of the species can grow to the size of a mouse and weigh more than 70 gm (2.5 oz). This is the heaviest insect in the world. It has a body length of around 20 cm (8 in.).

Weta

180   240 miles

300   400 kilometres

Takah

There are four species of New Zealand primitive frogs. Two of the species are classed as vulnerable in conservation terms, one as endangered and one as critical. There are no snakes in New Zealand.

The Takah – or South Island Takah – is a flightless bird found only in New Zealand. It was thought to be extinct but was rediscovered in 1948.

The world's longest name

Tetaumatawhakatangihangakoauaotamateaurehaeaturipuk apihimaungahoronukupokaiwhenuaakitanarahu is listed in the Guinness Book of Records as being the longest place name in the world. It's the name of a hill in Hawkes Bay in New Zealand. It means 'The brow of the hill, where Tamatea, the man with the big knees, who slid down, climbed up and swallowed'.

North America

Nort America is a continent bordered by the Arctic Ocean to the north, by the Atlantic Ocean to the east, by the Caribbean Sea to the southeast and by the Pacific Ocean to the south and west. It covers almost 5% of the Earth's surface – an area of about 24,480,000 sq km (9,450,000 sq miles). It is the third largest continent in area, with a population of more than 514,000,000.

The native people of North America originally came across the frozen Arctic Ocean from Asia, but centuries of immigration from Europe, Africa and south-east Asia have made the USA and Canada a multi-cultural society.

The American cordillera

This is a continuous string of mountains that stretches from Alaska to Antarctica. It includes ranges such as the Rocky Mountains in North America and the Andes in South America.

Rocky Mountains

The Rocky Mountains, or the Rockies, are part of a mountain chain that stretches more than 4,800 km (3,000 miles) from British Columbia in Canada to New Mexico in the United States. They contain ice caps, glaciers and volcanoes. The highest peak is Mount Elbert

ARCTIC OCEAN

ALASKA

Mt McKinley 29,322 ft ▲ (6,194 m) ● Anchorage

NORTH PACIFIC OCEAN

● Vancouver

Seattle

Win

San Francisco ●

● Los Angeles

C   A

U N I T E D
  O F   A M

Are the Great Lakes in the United States or Canada?

The five Great Lakes are on or near the United States / Canadian border. Lake Michigan is the only one entirely in the United States; it is the second largest in volume. The other four lakes are Lake Superior (the largest and deepest), Lake Huron (the second largest in area), Lake Erie (the smallest in volume and the shallowest) and Lake Ontario (the smallest in area). These four lakes form the border between the United States and Canada (the border runs roughly through the middle of the lakes).

Where is the coldest place in North America?

Yukon (Canada) and Greenland are among the world's coldest places, with temperatures reaching a low of –62°C (–80°F).

The world's biggest living tree is the giant Sequoia called General Sherman in the Sequoia National Park, California, standing 84 m (276 ft) tall, 11 m (36 ft) in diameter and with a girth of 31 m (102 ft).

In Canada the Inuit (formerly known as Eskimos) are able to govern themselves in the Nunavut province. They have adapted to the harsh environment and often combine modern technology with their traditional lifestyle.

fascinating facts

in Colorado, which is 4,401 m (14,440 ft) above sea level. Mount Robson, at 3,954 m (12,972 ft), is the highest peak in the Canadian Rockies.

Alaska

Alaska was part of Russia until 1867, when it was bought by the USA for £3.9 million (US$7.2 million). The America people thought it a waste of money, not knowing of the vast oil and gold reserves at the time!

More than 90 languages are spoken in Alaska.

Greenland

Greenland is the world's largest island. Although it is geographically part of the Arctic nation and therefore associated with North America, it is actually part of Europe. It has close ties to Europe politically and historically and is now a self-governed Danish territory. The people from Greenland live mainly in the coastal region, as ice sheet covers 80% of the island. The Vikings landed on Greenland in the 10th century having sailed from Iceland. By the 18th century it had come under Danish rule and became fully integrated into Denmark in 1953. 1n 1979 it became self-governing and in 1997 Inuit place names superseded Danish ones.

Old Faithful

The Old Faithful Geyser in Yellowstone National Park, USA, is probably the world's most famous geyser. An eruption can shoot up to 39 l (68 pints) of boiling water to a height of up to 55m (180 ft).

GREENLAND
(Kalaallit Nunaat)

Arctic Circle

◼ Nuuk (Godhaab)

A D A

St John's ●

Ottawa
◼

Chicago ●

New York ●

T A T E S

◼ Washington

I C A

Miami ●

300   600   900   1200 miles

500   1000   1500   2000 kilometres

Olympic Games

I n ancient times the Olympic Games were held in a place called Olympia, on the south-western Greek mainland. No one knows exactly when they were first held, but from 776 BC the Greeks started making a note of the date for the Games. The Olympic Games were held in honour of Zeus, the king of the gods.

At first only one race (the sprint) was run, and the Games lasted one day. Gradually more events were added, and by the end of the 5th century BC the Games lasted for five days. Only Greek male citizens were allowed to compete in the Games.

The festival

By the 1st century AD, Olympia had been transformed by the construction of magnificent stone temples and sports facilities. Two days before the start of the Olympic festival all the participants set out from Elis to walk 58 km (36 miles) to Olympia. This route was called the Sacred Way.

There were no awards for second or third place, but the winner received a wreath woven from a branch of the sacred olive tree in the Altis. This holy place was where the ancient Greeks believed the god Zeus lived in his great temple. The religious ending to the festival was the sacrifice to Zeus of 100 oxen.

Q&A?

Do you know why the Olympic flag has five rings?

The rings on the Olympic flag stand for the world's five continents, which are linked together by competing in the multi-national games.

Which swimmer holds the record for winning the most gold medals at one Olympic Games?

The American Mark Spitz holds the record. He won seven golds in swimming events at the 1972 Munich Games.

Banning the games

The Games gradually became more about pleasing the spectators than the gods. The final Olympic festival was held when the Christian Emperor of Rome, Theodosius I, banned the worship of non-Christian gods.

The Olympics were revived in June 1896 by Baron Pierre de Coubertin, who believed passionately that international sports competitions were a way to build friendship between nations.

The modern games

In 1896, nearly 250 men from different countries completed against one another for ten days and in 43 events. The modern Olympics are not religious and, since 1900, women have been allowed to take part.

The Paralympics

Since 1960 there has been a third kind of Olympics – for less able athletes. These Games are called the Paralympics, and they take place every four years, about the same time as the Summer Olympics. Paralympic events include all sorts of sports, from basketball to rhythmic gymnastics.

The marathon

The longest Olympic running race is the marathon. Athletes have to complete a course of about 42 km (26 miles). The event is named after a great Greek victory over Persian invaders in 490 BC. According to a later legend, a Greek messenger ran all the way from Marathon to Athens with the joyful news, then dropped dead.

fascinating facts

At the 1988 Paralympic Games, held at Seoul in South Korea, Denmark's wheelchair athlete Connie Hansen won five events. She was first in the 400 m, 800 m, 1500 m, 5,000 m and wheelchair marathon races. At the next Paralympics in 1992, in Barcelona, Spain, she won the marathon again!

Since the Amsterdam Games in 1928, a special flame burns at all Olympic venues. Since 1936 this flame has been brought from Olympia in Greece, and is usually carried by torch-bearers.

Pacific Ocean

The Pacific Ocean is the largest ocean in the world, covering 65% of the Earth's surface. At almost 70 million sq miles (180 million sq km), it is considerably larger than the entire land area of the whole world!

The Pacific Ocean stretches from the Arctic Circle to Antarctica, and from the western coasts of North and South America across thousands of small islands to New Zealand, Australia, Japan and mainland Asia.

How deep is the Pacific Ocean?

The average depth of the Pacific Ocean is 4,637.5 m (15,215 ft) deep. At its deepest part, the Mariana Trench, it is 11,034 m (36,200 ft) deep.

Does the International Date Line change in the Pacific Ocean?

Yes, it travels roughly along 180° longitude, with diversions to pass around some countries or islands. The International Date Line is an imaginary line that separates two consecutive days. The date in the Eastern Hemisphere is always one day ahead of the date in the Western Hemisphere.

Peaceful sea?

Pacific is from the Latin words for 'Peace.' However the Pacific is not always peaceful. Many typhoons pound the islands of the Pacific. The area is full of volcanoes and often affected by earthquakes. Tsunamis, caused by underwater earthquakes, have damaged islands and destroyed entire towns and communities. Massive whirls, formed by ocean currents, are found in the area north and south of the equator.

Fishing

The main fishing areas in the Pacific are found in the more shallow waters of the continental shelf. The continental shelf is the extended land beyond each continent, which is relatively shallow. Then comes the continental slope, which eventually merges into the deep ocean floor. Salmon, halibut, herring, sardines and tuna are the chief catch. Not all fishing communities have large commercial fleets, however. Small island communities fish nearer to home.

Exploration and settlement

The first people who lived on the islands were from Asia. They crossed the open seas in ancient boats. Europeans explorers arrived in the 16th century, people such as Vasco Núñez de Balboa from Spain. During the 17th century the Dutchman Abel Janszoon Tasman discovered Tasmania

and New Zealand. Then the 18th century saw the Russians land in Alaska, and the French settle in Polynesia. The British sailed with Captain James Cook to Australia, the South Pacific, Hawaii, and North American.

The Pacific is rich in mineral wealth, but the ocean is so deep that mining would be very difficult and dangerous. In the shallower waters of the continental shelves off the coasts of Australia and New Zealand, petroleum and natural gas are extracted, and pearls are harvested along the coasts of Australia, Japan, Papua New Guinea and the Philippines.

During the 1800s Charles Darwin's research on his five-year voyage on the HMS Beagle brought him fame as a geologist and author. He studied the theory of evolution and natural selection. In 1859 he published the book *On the Origin of Species*. Many of the animals he studied can still be seen in the Pacific, in particular the turtles and tortoises of the Galapagos Islands.

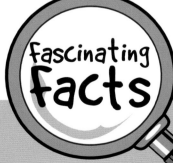

Fascinating Facts

90% of all volcanic activity occurs in the oceans.

If you placed Mount Everest in the Marianas Trench there would still be over 1.6 km (a mile) of ocean above it.

Plants *and* trees

There are a huge variety of plants and trees. Plants and trees take up water and nutrients from soil through their roots. The green colouring in leaves and stems is called chlorophyll. It is important for photosynthesis – the process by which plants make sugar from carbon dioxide and water. The sugar is then used by the plant as energy for growth.

Plants and trees are essential because they take in carbon dioxide to use in photosynthesis and a product of photosynthesis is oxygen, which we need to breathe.

Some trees and shrubs are evergreen – they keep their leaves all year. Others are deciduous – their leaves fall off in autumn.

Many trees and plants are well adapted for the situation in which they grow. For example, fir trees have narrow, tough, needle-like leaves that can withstand very cold weather. Plants that grow in hot, dry places have small leaves or a very tough coating – like cacti. This ensures that they can live off small amounts of water.

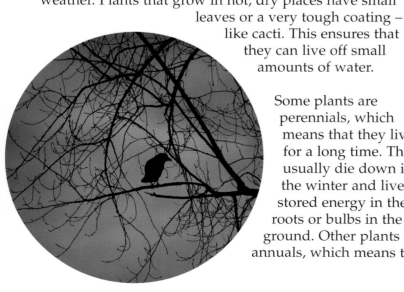

Some plants are perennials, which means that they live for a long time. They usually die down in the winter and live off stored energy in their roots or bulbs in the ground. Other plants are annuals, which means that they grow, flower and set seed in one season. At the end of the summer the plant dies and the seeds are scattered.

New plants can be made in two ways – by vegetative propagation (where new plants grow without seeds or spores) or by sowing seeds.

Trees and plants have many uses:

- Cereals such as wheat, rice, oats, barley and maize are grown around the world for food.

- Drinks – coffee comes from roasted coffee beans, chocolate from cacao seeds, and tea from dried leaves of the tea plant.

- Construction materials, such as wood from trees and thatch from reeds.

- Cotton fibres for cloth.

- Rope is made from hemp.

- Drugs and medicines – opium for controlling pain comes from poppies, digitalis for heart disease comes from foxgloves, and drugs made from chemicals extracted from periwinkles and yew trees are used for cancer.

The tallest trees in the world are the giant redwoods of California which are more than 100 m (330 ft) metres tall.

Tree roots can be so strong that they can split rocks and sometime damage roads and walls.

Horsetail was around at the time of the dinosaurs. We know this because it's been found in dinosaur fossils. It grows almost everywhere in the world except Australia and Antarctica.

The biggest flower in the world (*Rafflesia arnoldii*) is found in the Indonesian jungle. It can grow to be 0.9 m (3 ft) across and weigh up to 6.8 kg (15 lb). It smells of rotting meat and this attracts insects, which pollinate it when they walk across it searching for the meat which they think they can smell.

 Fascinating Facts

Some plants protect themselves from being eaten by animals by growing thorns or spikes along their stems or having parts which are poisonous. Yew trees are poisonous in all parts except for the fleshy red coating of their berries.

Dendrochronology is a method of finding out the age of a tree by tree-ring dating, Trees grow a new ring each year. Wide rings often show a year of good growth when water and nutrients were plentiful but a narrow ring indicates a difficult year, sometimes when there was a drought.

 Q&A?

Can plants be carnivorous?

Some plants live in such poor soil that they have become carnivorous. An example is the Venus Fly Trap – they get some of their nutrients by catching and digesting insects.

What is a parasitic plant?

A parasitic plant is one that takes some or all of its food from another plant (the host). Mistletoe is a parasitic plant; it has no roots of its own, it grows on certain trees and it sucks its nutrients from the host tree.

Prehistory

Prehistory, or 'before history', is the period of human evolution before written records. Palaeontologists study fossils, tools and paintings to work out how people lived.

Prehistory is divided into three broad ages of prehistoric people: Stone Age, Bronze Age and Iron Age. These names are based on the technology used during the different periods. New artefacts (objects) are still being discovered, providing new information about what the world was like for early human beings.

The Stone Age

The Stone Age or 'Neolithic' period was 2 million years ago. Tools and weapons were made from stone, and people hunted animals, fished with simple weapons, gathered food such as berries from plants, and discovered fire.

Archaeologists have found cave paintings, which show that early people produced artwork, such as rock paintings called 'petroglyphs'. Early humans also used dyes to decorate their bodies, and there is evidence that some of them used copper ore to produce basic tools. Very hard rocks like flint were shaped to use as cutting tools or arrowheads. There was an increasing use of technology, and a gradual development of agriculture. Dogs were used for hunting, and lived with their masters.

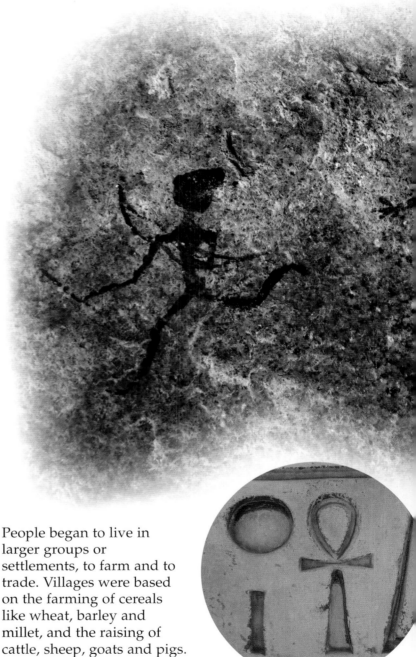

People began to live in larger groups or settlements, to farm and to trade. Villages were based on the farming of cereals like wheat, barley and millet, and the raising of cattle, sheep, goats and pigs.

The Bronze Age

The Bronze Age in Britain is considered to have been from around 2100 BC to 700 BC. Metalworking began during this period, and bronze tools were increasingly common and useful. There was skilled and detailed workmanship, producing many beautiful objects such as carved drinking horns and decorated pottery. There were also some early forms of writing, such as Egyptian hieroglyphs and Mayan symbols.

The first use of iron occurred in Ancient Egypt around 4000 BC. Spear tips and beads were fashioned from iron found in meteorites.

Skara Brae on the island of Orkney, off the coast of Scotland, is a Neolithic village discovered by archaeologists. Here archaeologists found stone beds and shelves, and even an indoor toilet connected to a nearby stream.

A cave painting

The search for more raw materials led to exploration and colonisation of new territories. Trade routes enabled travellers to reach other countries. Cities were formed and countries emerged, but traders became rivals and competition for raw materials led to wars. Communities built boats, developed farming techniques and invented new technology, for example the ox-drawn plough.

The Iron Age

The Iron Age in Britain is considered to have been from around 5th century BC until the Roman conquest in England and until the 5th century AD in other parts of Britain. Iron tools and weapons were made in this period, which ended with the development of written history. Different parts of the world advanced at different speeds. The Greek and Roman Empires and their great cultures were very advanced, but in Northern Europe the Iron Age lasted until the early Middle Ages.

Iron was hard, had a high melting point, and there was a lot of iron ore available. So having once been rare and costly, iron was now a cheap and useful material, and became used for many different tasks.

Iron allowed warfare to become more sophisticated. There was fighting on horseback and in horse-drawn chariots, and swords and arrows were produced from iron.

Coins were manufactured in bronze, making trade easier. Iron-made tools were stronger and better, and people's lives improved because of higher agricultural productivity. Iron-tipped ploughs were more efficient than wooden ones, and iron axes cut down trees quickly – clearing land for farming, and providing wood for building.

What was the most important invention of the Bronze age?

The wheel. This allowed people to make carts and transport goods.

How is bronze made?

Bronze is a mixture of copper, tin and other metals.

Rainforests

Rainforests are lush green jungles, with incredibly tall trees and hot, humid climates. They are called 'rainforests' because they get rain almost every single day. More than 50% of this rainfall is water that has evaporated from the rainforest itself and then cooled and condensed back into rain.

The animals and plants that live in the rainforests have adapted to the extremely hot and humid conditions there. Although rainforests cover only 6% of the Earth's surface, they are home to more than half the world's animal and plant species!

Plants layers in a rainforest

Top layer – formed of giant trees up to 75 m (246 ft) tall. Only 1% of trees grow high enough to reach this layer. Animals here tend to be strong fliers like bats, macaws, eagles – even some butterflies!

Canopy layer – the main part of the rainforest, formed of smaller trees, 20–30 m (66–98 ft) tall. It receives full sunlight, and in many places the branches form a leafy 'canopy' which prevents sunlight and rain getting to lower levels. This layer teems with life – good climbers such as monkeys, snakes and lemurs can be found here, as well as birds such as toucans and hornbills.

Where are rainforests?

Rainforests are found in 85 countries near the equator – in Central America, Africa, Australia and Asia. Central America was once covered with rainforest, but large areas have now been cleared.

Which is the largest rainforest?

The world's largest rainforest is the Amazon jungle in South America, covering 6,992,968 sq m (2,700,000 sq miles).

Understory – the dark layer beneath the canopy where only 2% of light gets through! Plants here are much smaller – woody vines, small trees and tall shrubs. Most animals here live on the trees, like spiders, insects, small mammals and frogs.

Forest floor – the lowest layer, the floor of the rainforest. Little vegetation grows here. The main animals down here are large mammals like gorillas, aardvarks and jaguars, and insects like ants and beetles.

Animal life

There are millions, perhaps billions, of animals living inside the rainforests. About 90% are insects. Other common animals are reptiles such as lizards and snakes, tropical birds such as toucans and parrots, and other mammals such as monkeys, leopards and sloths. Animals have adapted to live in the rainforests through camouflage, slowness, disguise and poison. Animals like chameleons and stick insects use camouflage to blend in with the leaves and trees, making them hard to see.

Sloths have adapted to move slowly because that saves energy in the heat and makes it harder for predators to see them. Animals use disguise to make predators think they are bigger or more dangerous than they really are – some butterflies have markings that look like eyes on their wings, to appear like the head of a bigger animal. Poison is used as a defence and for capturing prey. The poison-arrow frog has brightly coloured and patterned bodies as a warning to predators – which says 'don't eat me, I'm poisonous!'.

Rainforests at risk

Wide areas of rainforest are being cut down – the equivalent of 4,000 football pitches every hour! Rare animals and plants now face extinction and the tribes who live there may have lost their homes.

Plant life

Rainforests teem with plant life – many plants have also adapted to thrive in their surroundings.

Rainforest plants

Lianas – these are rope-like vines which grow up trees towards the sunlight. Once at the top of the canopy, they spread to other trees.

'Pitcher' Plants – these carnivorous plants are named after their jug-shaped leaves. Inside these leaves is a strong smelling nectar that attracts insects, which get trapped inside the leaves and are then digested by the plant. Pitcher plants can be up to 9 m (30 ft) tall.

Bromeliads – these pineapple-like plants have thick waxy leaves which form a bowl shape and catch water. Some hold several gallons, and have been found with creatures like frogs and snails living inside them.

Plants that grow on trees – many rainforest plants actually grow on the branches and trunks of trees, where there is more light and air than on the forest floor. These sunlight-loving plants are called epiphytes – some examples are orchids.

Reptiles

Reptile comes from the Latin 'reper' meaning to creep. Historically, reptiles were defined as cold-blooded, scaled animals, but scientists have now replaced this definition with a broader one. The big difference is that birds are now seen as reptiles because they evolved from dinosaurs, which were reptiles.

There are four main groups of reptile: Crocodilia, Rhynchocephalia, Squamataand Testudines.

Crocodilia

This group includes crocodiles, caimans and alligators. Their name comes from the Greek krokodeilos, meaning pebble worm. The first crocodilians evolved 220 million years ago. Crocodilians, along with sharks, are sometimes referred to as 'living fossils' because unlike most other animals they have remained unchanged for millions of years.

Iguana

Rhyncocephalia

The only surviving members of this group, the tuatara, are native to New Zealand. The name tuatara comes from the native Maori language and means 'peaks on the back', referring to the spiny ridges running down their back. The most striking difference from other reptiles is their teeth: tuatara have two rows of teeth in their upper jaw and a single row in their lower jaw which fits between the two upper rows. When the tuatara closes its mouth, the interlocking teeth enable it to tear apart hard insects and other prey.

Squamata

This is the largest group of modern reptiles, with over 7,600 known species. It includes snakes, lizards and limbless reptiles (amphisbaenia).

Tuatara

Snakes

'Snake' comes from the Old English 'snaca', meaning to crawl. They have long, narrow bodies covered in fine scales. As the snake grows it sheds its old skin in one piece, emerging with a fresh one.

Snakes' eyes are protected by transparent scales called 'spectacle' scales. They don't have ears but hear through small bones under the skin. They smell by flicking their forked tongue, sampling tiny particles in the air and passing them back to a sensitive organ at the back of the mouth.

Some snakes, like the Black Mamba, have a poisonous bite. Others, like the boa constrictor, wrap themselves around

Crocodile

90

Today reptiles can be found on every continent except Antarctica.

Snakes are covered by a plates and scales that are nearly watertight. Even their eyes are covered by clear scales to keep the dirt out!

Fascinating Facts

Slow worm

Amphisbaenia

These 'worm lizards' are a rare group of limbless reptiles which resemble scaly worms and live in warm or tropical regions. Their skulls are wide and blend seamlessly into the body, their eyes and ears are concealed under a covering of fine scales, and they have a short blunt tail.

Corn snake

their prey and crush it to death by squeezing or 'constricting' it. Others swallow their prey whole.

Snakes can swallow much larger creatures than seems possible, because they have a flexible lower jaw that allows them to open their mouths very wide.

Lizards

Lizards are scaled, usually four-legged, and have external ear openings and movable eyelids. Many can shed their tail when attacked, hopefully distracting the predator and allowing the lizard to escape. The tail later regrows. Some lizards, like the chameleon, can change colour in response to their surroundings. Most lizards feed on insects and rodents but some, like the iguana, are herbivores which only eat plants.

Testudines

Testudines, or turtles, are a line of reptiles that dates back over 250 million years, much earlier than snakes and lizards. They have large, hard shells that protect their bodies leaving only their head, limbs and tail exposed. Today they include tortoises, marine turtles like the one shown above and terrapins.

Q&A?

What does cold-blooded mean?

The term cold-blooded is a bit misleading because a reptile's blood is not cold. But reptiles don't generate enough heat from their own bodies to maintain a constant blood temperature (as mammals, including humans, do). Instead reptiles rely on their environment and behaviour to maintain their body temperature. They bask in the sun to warm themselves up, and move into the shade to avoid overheating.

Which were the earliest reptiles?

The earliest reptiles are believed to be creatures called Hylonomus. They were a small, lizard-like creature that lived about 315 million years ago, long before the first dinosaurs.

The Romans

Around 2,000 years ago, the Roman Empire dominated Europe. It ruled lands around the Mediterranean from France to Turkey to North Africa. It came to an end in 476 AD.

The city of Rome

Rome was the capital city of the Roman Empire, and today is the capital city of Italy. It was famous for being built on seven hills. At first, Rome was ruled by kings, but the last king, Tarquin the Proud, was overthrown in 510 BC and Rome became a Republic. A republic is a form of government that is not ruled by a monarch (king or queen). The Republic was ruled for 400 years by a council called the Senate.

The Roman army

Over time, the generals of the Roman army became very powerful, and started to control government. However, they tended to argue among themselves, and eventually just one man took over – Rome had an Emperor.

The Romans were able to keep and expand their Empire thanks to their army. They had the first professional army of paid soldiers in the world. Soldiers were brought into the army from all parts of the Empire, and sent to fight far away from their homes. The army was organised as follows:

- The army was divided into legions of 5,000 men. There were about 30 legions.
  - Each legion was divided into ten cohorts.
  - Each cohort was divided into six centuries. A century contained 80 men and was commanded by an officer called a Centurion.
  - Each century was divided into ten groups of eight men who lived, travelled and fought together.

What did a Roman soldier wear?

The Roman soldiers were very well-equipped. Ordinary soldiers wore leather sandals, wool tunics and leather breeches. They had armour made from overlapping iron bands. They carried a curved shield (called a scutum) and had a bronze helmet. Each man carried a sword (called a gladius), two javelins and a dagger.

Roman towns

The Romans built towns in all the lands they conquered. They were all built to the same plan. Streets were arranged in a criss-cross pattern. Two main streets divided the town, with smaller streets built off them at right angles.

Q&A?

What did Roman women wear?

Roman women wore a garment called a stola, a long dress of fine woollen cloth that came to their ankles. They often wore their hair curled and up on top of their heads, and were fond of jewellery.

What did the Roman men wear?

Roman men wore knee-length tunics, belted at the waist, and sandals. For important occasions they would wear a toga, a drape of fine wool cloth that went around and over the body, covering the right shoulder.

Amphitheatre – where public entertainments like gladiator contests and chariot races were held. There is a picture of one at the top of page 164.

Amphitheatre – where public entertainments like gladiator contests and chariot races were held. There is a picture of one at the top of page 164.

Basilica – this was something like the town hall, where government took place.

Roman engineering

Central heating – public baths and the houses of rich people had central heating! Floors were built on top of a series of 'tunnels' called a hypocaust – hot air from a furnace travelled through these tunnels, heating the floors and rooms above.

Plumbing – Roman houses had the best drains in the ancient world. Underground drains took away waste water and sewage, and were flushed through with water from the baths.

Aqueducts – Roman towns had piped water. If water had to be brought from a long way away, they would build huge aqueducts (a kind of bridge that carried water on the top of it) across valleys.

Roads – long, straight 'Roman roads' were built wherever the Romans went, and many can still be seen today.

fascinating facts

The first Roman Emperor was called Augustus. He came to power in 27 BC.

Walls were built round the town for protection, and people could only enter or leave by gates.

Rich people lived in well-built town houses, but poor people lived in cheap blocks of apartments, some up to four storeys high. Rich houses had central heating, plumbing, gardens and lovely decorations like mosaic floors.

The Roman town

You could find the following buildings in any Roman town:

Forum – Important buildings like offices and law courts were built around this 'town square', and a market was often held here.

Baths – the Romans built large public bathhouses called thermae. People went there to get clean but also to relax and meet friends. As well as bathing, they could exercise there in the gymnasium.

The solar system

The sun, the centre of our solar system, is a giant, spinning ball of very hot gas. The light from the sun heats our world and makes life possible. The solar system consists of the sun and nine planets (and their moons) which orbit the sun. Scientists study the planets and stars with very sophisticated equipment, such as radio telescopes and satellites.

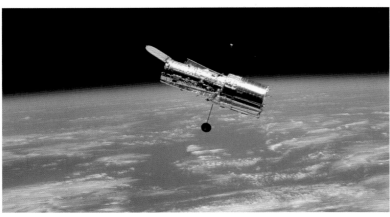

A satellite

The planets

The inner planets (those planets that orbit close to the sun) are quite different from the outer planets (those planets that orbit far away from the sun).

The inner planets

Mercury, Venus, Earth and Mars are the inner planets. They are relatively small, composed mostly of rock, and have few or no moons.

Mercury is the closest planet to the sun and is the fastest-moving planet. Temperatures on Mercury range between 400°C and –170°C (750°F and –274°F).

Venus is a similar size to the Earth; it is the brightest and, at 475°C (887°F), the hottest of the planets, due to its atmosphere of carbon dioxide gas which traps the sun's energy. Scientists have tried to send probes onto this scorching planet, but the atmosphere has proved too hot.

Earth looks blue and white from space due to the oceans and clouds which cover its surface. It consists of a solid crust above a molten layer, at the centre of which is a solid iron core. Earth is surrounded by a layer of gases which form an atmosphere, and 71% of its surface is covered with liquid water – a property unique in the Solar System and which has enabled life to develop. The Earth is 152 million km (94.5 million miles) from the sun.

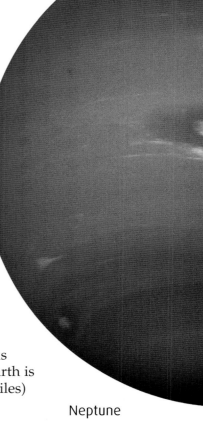

Neptune

Mars also has an atmosphere and has, in the past, had water, leading to theories that there might be life on Mars. Space probes have tested the surface and found no trace of life.

The outer planets are Jupiter, Saturn, Uranus, Neptune and Pluto. They are mostly very large, mostly gaseous, ringed and have many moons. Pluto is the exception – it is small, rocky and has one moon.

The largest planet, **Jupiter,** consists of hydrogen and helium and is covered by clouds.

Saturn is famous for its rings, which are 270,000 km (167,000 miles) across but only 200 m (660 ft) thick. The rings are made of chunks of ice varying from snowball to iceberg size.

Uranus is a very cold planet, as it is 20 times further from the heat of the sun than the Earth.

Very little was known about **Neptune** until the *Voyager 2* spacecraft showed pictures of its blue-green clouds.

Pluto is the smallest, coldest and most distant planet in the Solar System. It was only discovered in 1930. Surface temperatures are –233°C (–387.5°F).

Stars

A star is an enormous ball of gas. It generates energy and therefore emits light. All stars except the sun appear as tiny shining points

Q&A?

Is the moon a planet?

No. The moon is Earth's natural satellite. It is a cold, dry orb whose surface is covered with craters and scattered with rocks and dust. The moon has no atmosphere. It is possible that there is some frozen ice on the moon.

Do stars last forever?

The average life span of a yellow star, like the sun, is about 10 billion years. The sun will eventually burn out in about 5 to 6 billion years.

in the night sky that twinkle because of the effect of the Earth's atmosphere and their distance from us. The sun is also a star and although only a medium-sized one, it is close enough to Earth to appear as a disk and to provide daylight.

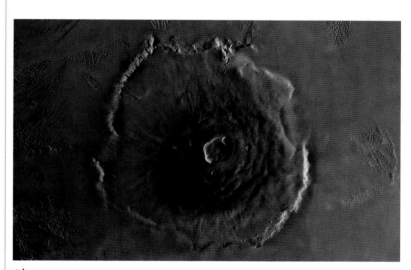

Olympus Mons

Viewed edge-on, Saturn's rings seem to disappear. Jupiter, Uranus and Neptune also have rings, but these are much fainter.

Mars is the home of Olympus Mons, the largest volcano found in the solar system. It stands about 27 km (17 miles) high with a crater 50 miles (81 km) wide.

Fascinating Facts

The solar system

Space travel

Rockets have interested scientists and amateurs for at least 2,100 years. The Chinese used them as weapons as early as the 11th century.

In the 1880s Russian scientist Konstantin Tsiolkovsky worked out that for a rocket to escape the Earth's gravity (the force that pulls objects back to the ground), it would have to travel at a speed of 8 km (5 miles) a second and that to achieve this, a multi-stage rocket fuelled by liquid oxygen and liquid hydrogen was needed.

However, it was not until 1926 that the American Robert Goddard designed a liquid fuel rocket that would actually work. At the time, though, Goddard's work was laughed at. It was only later, when people realised that rocket technology could be used in weapons, that his work was taken seriously.

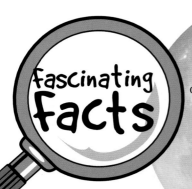

fascinating facts

Sputnik means 'satellite' (an object that circles the earth, as the moon does) and also 'fellow traveller' in Russian.

During the Apollo 14 mission, astronaut Alan Shepard hit three golf balls on the surface of the moon – they are still there!

Why were the first American spaceships called Apollo?

They were named after Apollo, the Greek and Roman god of the sun.

What is the International Space Station?

The space station that is being built in space allows people to live and study for long periods in a 'weightless' environment, and to understand the effects of gravity on plants, animals, and humans. It isn't finished yet, but it's already the largest synthetic object in space, measuring about 120 m x 96 m (390 ft x 315 ft) and has lots of solar panels to provide electricity.

The space race

Both the Soviet Union and America wanted to be the first to send satellites, rockets, and men into space. The Soviets had the first successes. On 4 October 1957, they successfully launched Sputnik 1 and the space race began. Because it showed that the Soviets might be capable of using space technology to make weapons, and because it showed that their country had enough money to build expensive spacecraft, Sputnik caused fear in the United States. At the same time, the Sputnik launch was seen in the Soviet Union as an important sign of the strength of the nation. Before Sputnik, America had assumed that it was better than other countries at everything. After Sputnik, they launched a huge effort to get ahead in the space race.

The imagination of the American public was captured by the American space projects. School children followed the launches, and making model rockets became a popular hobby. President Kennedy gave speeches encouraging people to support the space programme. Nearly four months after the launch of Sputnik 1, the US launched its first satellite, Explorer I. But before this there were lots of embarrassing launch failures at Cape Canaveral!

Animals and humans in space

In 1957 the dog Laika was sent into orbit in the Soviet's Sputnik 2. The technology to bring her back did not exist, so she died in space. The American space program then sent chimpanzees into space before launching their first human orbiter. The cosmonaut (Soviet astronaut) Yuri Gagarin became the first man in space when he entered orbit in the Soviet's Vostok 1 on 12 April 1961, and 23 days later, Alan Shepard first entered space for the United States. John Glenn, in Friendship 7, became the first American to successfully orbit Earth, completing three orbits on 20 February 1962. Soviet Valentina Tereshkova became the first woman in space on 16 June 1963 in Vostok 6.

Man on the moon

The Americans felt that the only way to win the space race was to put a man on the moon. President John Kennedy said, 'We choose to go to the moon. We choose to go to the moon in this decade and do the other things, not because they are easy, but because they are hard.' It was an American, Neil Armstrong, who became the first person to set foot on the moon's surface on 21 July 1969, after landing in Apollo 11 the previous day. It was an event watched on television by over 500 million people around the world. It was one of the finest moments of the 20th century, and Armstrong's words on his first touching the moon's surface have become very famous: 'That's one small step for man, one giant leap for mankind.'

Advances in space

There have been many missions into space and to the moon since Neil Armstrong took his famous first steps. America and the Soviet Union have launched space stations into Earth's orbit, and there are plans for an international space station. The Hubble Space Telescope was launched in 1990 and the pictures it has taken of deep space are very clear and have shown many exciting new things. Astronauts also carry out lots of new experiments on every mission to see how things react differently in space from here on Earth.

Towns *and* cities

In ancient times, people lived mainly in small communities in villages or hamlets. The earliest towns were often built near rivers so that people could get water to drink and fish to eat. When the Romans occupied countries, they built towns, castles and walls for protection. They linked towns by building straight roads, some of which still exist today!

Early towns

In many countries, the rich and wealthy lords and landowners lived in castles or manor houses. Other people lived in small houses, and would sell their goods in local markets. Early towns began to develop around these markets, and people would buy and sell the things they could not make or grow themselves.

Where does the word 'city' come from?

It comes from the Latin word civitas, meaning 'citizenship or community of citizens'. The Latin word for city was urbs, and a resident of a city was a civis.

What is the largest capital city in Europe?

Moscow (Russia) is the largest, with more than 8 million people.

The growth of the towns

Towns often developed around ports and harbours, where people traded by boat and ship. Some of these harbour towns exist today, and trade still goes on in them. Other early towns were built on hilltops so that people could watch out for any approaching enemy. Many medieval towns had walls, and people could live inside the walls for safety. Originally, the word town meant a fortified place (somewhere with a wall or some defences). Most walled towns were dirty and smelly places – there was little sanitation (ways to make things clean) and no running water or soap. That caused disease and illness, and people in those days did not live very long.

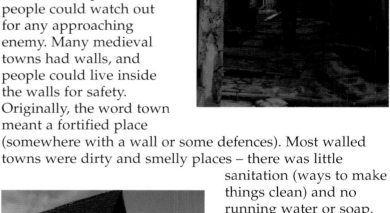

The move to the cities

Early methods of farming were fairly basic and did not produce much food. Then as farming methods improved more food could be grown on the same amount of land. Better farming methods meant that fewer people were needed and so people moved to the cities.

Town or city?

A city is usually a big urban area with a large population, but in some countries the word 'city' has a particular meaning. In Britain, for example, a place with a cathedral is a city, even if it is quite small. In medieval times, many British cities, including York, Lincoln and Canterbury, became important because of their cathedrals. In the United States, many small population areas are also called 'cities' because they have been given the legal status of cities by the government. In most countries, however, a city means a place with a very big urban core and large population.

The industrial revolution

Up until the 1800s, people in most countries produced goods by hand, using skills learnt from their elders. After the Industrial Revolution, which began in Britain and spread throughout the world, goods could be produced cheaply and quickly in factories because newly developed machinery could do the work of many people. This caused anger among craftsmen because it took work away from them.

Cities today

Today there are many big cities in the world. Some of the largest are Mumbai, Tokyo, Shanghai and Seoul in Asia; Cairo and Lagos in Africa; Moscow and London in Europe; Mexico City and New York in North America; and Sao Paulo in South America. Modern methods of transport have made it easier to travel quickly between cities. Also, modern methods of communication such as telephone and email allow people to communicate instantly. Nowadays fewer people have to go into a town to work than in the recent past – some people can even stay at home and work through the Internet! Modern working methods have meant that many people no longer have to live in towns or cities.

The most populous city (the one with the largest number of people) in the world is Shanghai, China, with a population of more than 15 million!

The term 'City of London' refers to a small area in central London. It is approximately 2.6 sq km (1 sq mile) and is London's main financial centre. Modern London developed from the original City of London and the nearby City of Westminster, where the royal government was located.

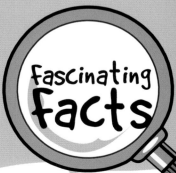

fascinating Facts

Travel *and* transport

Before the invention of the wheel, people had to carry their belongings themselves, or pull them on wooden sledges. Carts with stone wheels arrived around 3,500 BC, and later horses pulled the carts. Iron horseshoes weren't developed until around 770 AD. This made horse power much more efficient as the iron shoes prevented the horse's hooves from being worn away by walking over rough roads.

The Romans built roads – some of the routes of the Roman roads are still in use today!

Over the centuries farmers and merchants continued to use carts to transport goods, and people began to use four-wheeled carriages. However, these were only available to the rich until the arrival of the omnibus, or bus as we call them today. The first bus route, schedule (timetable) and fare system was invented in France in 1662 by the mathematician Blaise Pascal, but buses did not become common until the late 1700s.

People travelled by water along rivers or over seas and lakes. This was done by wind power (using sails) and people power (using oars). The first canoes were invented around 3,500 BC and the Ancient Egyptians used large boats to move goods down the Nile. The Romans used ships to travel to other lands and expand their empire, using slaves for their rowing power. Over time bigger and better sailing ships were designed. During the Age of Discovery in the 15th and 16th centuries, European explorers sailed across the oceans in huge galleons. Inland, miles and miles of canals (constructed waterways) were built in the 18th and 19th centuries throughout Europe to transport goods to and from the coast and between cities.

Great changes came when people began to invent machine-powered transportation. This used steam power from burning wood or coal. People could transport goods much more quickly, which was good for business. Later, mechanical means of transportation meant that individual people could travel from place to place and could see the world easily and affordably.

The first steamboat with a regular passenger service was invented by Robert Fulton in 1807. Nowadays steam power has been replaced by diesel fuel, and passenger ships are mostly car ferries or holiday cruise ships. Ships still transport goods across the oceans, but mostly in containers. The first steam powered locomotive (train) was invented by Richard Trevithick in 1801 but it was designed to go on

The artist and inventor Leonardo da Vinci sketched a bicycle as early as 1490. He also made over 100 drawings of his theories of flight, sketching flying machines like the ornithopter, and drew a design for a motorised carriage.

An early bicycle was invented in 1790 by Comte Mede de Sivrac, but unfortunately it had no steering!

the roads! The first steam-powered railroad locomotive was George Stevenson's *Rocket*, invented in 1814.

The 19th century was the age of railroad building in Europe and America. The railway took over from the canals as the main method for transporting heavy goods such as coal.

Although a clockwork-powered carriage was invented in 1740, the world's first practical automobile was built in 1867. Henry Ford started the Ford Motor Company in 1903. He wanted to make the car for everyone, not just a luxury item for the extremely rich. Since then the car has become the most popular type of transport, as it is affordable and available to virtually everyone.

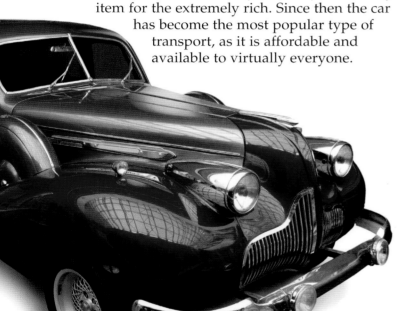

What was the Tin Lizzie?

It was a nickname for the Ford Model T. This car was launched in 1908 and during over 19 years nearly 15,500,000 were sold in the USA alone!

Who invented the hot-air balloon?

Joseph and Jacques Etienne Montgolfière were two French brothers who made the first successful hot-air balloon. Their first balloon was launched in December 1783, and ascended to an altitude of 300 m (985 ft). This type of hot-air balloon was called the Montgolfière; it was made of paper and used air heated by burning wool and moist straw.

A timeline of transport:

1783 ➜ The first hot-air balloon invented by the Montgolfière brothers.
1895 ➜ First human glider flown by Otto Lilienthal.
1899 ➜ The first successful airship, the Zeppelin, invented by Ferdinand von Zeppelin.
1903 ➜ The first airplane flown by the Wright brothers (first powered flight).
1907 ➜ First helicopter invented by Paul Cornu.
1926 ➜ First liquid-propelled rocket launched by Robert H. Goddard.
1940 ➜ Modern helicopters invented by Igor Sirkorsky.
1947 ➜ First supersonic (faster than the speed of sound) flight.
1967 ➜ First successful supersonic passenger jet (Concorde).
1969 ➜ First manned mission to the moon (Apollo 11).
1981 ➜ Space shuttle launched.

United Kingdom

The United Kingdom comprises Great Britain and Northern Ireland. Great Britain is Europe's largest island and for the last 500 years has been one of the world's most influential and richest countries. At its height the British Empire stretched over 25% of the Earth's surface, ruling countries such as Canada, South Africa, India and Australia, which is why so many nations in the world speak English. The Empire is no more, and Scotland, Wales and Northern Ireland now have their own parliaments.

The UK was a world leader in shipbuilding, steel making, car manufacturing and coal mining, but these have declined, with most people now employed in finance, health care, education, retail and tourism.

Languages

The language of the UK is predominantly English, although Welsh is spoken by 25% of the Welsh people and Gaelic is spoken to a lesser extent in Western Scotland and the Hebrides. Cornish is spoken in small areas of Cornwall. The UK is a multi-cultural society and many languages are spoken, mainly from the Indian subcontinent and Africa.

England

England is the largest of the British nations and has, in London, one of the most cosmopolitan capital cities in the world. It is home to both the government and the

monarchy and the headquarters of many national institutions and companies. This combination of royalty and national monuments attracts tourists from around the world. The most visited sights are Westminster Abbey, Downing Street and St Paul's Cathedral.

Northern Ireland

Northern Ireland consists of the six counties of Ulster and is situated in the north-east of Ireland. It covers 14,139 sq km (5,459 sq miles), about a sixth of the total area of the island. It is mostly rural with industry centred around the capital Belfast.

Northern Ireland's most spectacular feature is the Giant's Causeway (a causeway is a path). The unique rock formations have withstood Atlantic storms for millions of years. This feature is the result of volcanic activity. The Causeway itself is made up of hexagonal columns of differing heights. There are over 40,000 of these columns. The story is that the giant stepped from Ireland and over to Scotland, using the columns on Staffa (near Mull in the Scottish Highlands) as a stepping stone.

Giant's causeway

Was the Titanic built in the UK?

The **Titanic** *was built at the Harland and Wolff shipyard in Belfast, Northern Ireland. She was the largest passenger ship in the world. On April 14, 1912, she broke into two pieces, and sank two hours and forty minutes later at 2:20 a.m. Monday morning.*

Why doesn't the Queen rule England?

England (and the rest of the UK) has been ruled by a parliament of elected officials since the mid-13th century.

representatives who have total control over issues such as education, health, agriculture and justice. The parliament is in the capital city of Edinburgh, which has many fine buildings such as Edinburgh Castle and Holyrood House.

Wales

Successive English Kings tried to integrate Wales into England. King Edward I ordered a ring of castles to be built to circle the land but it was not until the reign of Henry VIII that Wales was fully intergrated. The castles today remain as magnificent tourist attractions. Wales is a rugged country; in the north are the magnificent mountains of Snowdonia. Mid Wales has a more rolling countryside but is very sparsely populated, while in the south are the Black Mountains and the coal-rich Welsh Valleys. It is in this region that the capital, Cardiff, is situated and where most of the people live.

Scotland

The Celts of Scotland have always fiercely defended their homeland. The Romans could not defeat them and built two walls, the Antonine Wall between the River Clyde and the Firth of Forth and Hadrian's Wall between the River Solway and River Tyne, to try and keep them out of England. The two countries became unified in 1707. The Scots achieved their own parliament in 1998 and elected

Stonehenge is a megalithic monument located in the English county of Wiltshire. It is composed of earthworks surrounding a circular setting of large standing stones and is one of the most famous prehistoric sites in the world. Archaeologists think thestanding stones were erected between 2500 and 2000 BC.

Britain is the home to the world's most poisonous fungus, the yellowish olive Death Cap.

Fascinating Facts

The USA

The USA stretches from the Arctic Ocean to tropical Hawaii and includes the massive Rocky Mountains as well as fertile lowlands. Vast natural resources and a culture of enterprise make the USA one of the world's richest nations, the home of many global businesses such as Ford, McDonald's, Microsoft and Disney.

The people

The United States has one of the world's most diverse populations, with immigrants from all over the world. Thousands of years ago, Asians crossed the Bering Strait from Asia and populated both North and South America. Their descendants are the Native Americans. Spanish, French and English settlers colonized in the 1600s, and slaves from Africa were brought to the country later. The Industrial Revolution attracted millions of European immigrants from Ireland, Britain and Italy, and the last 50 years have brought immigrants from Mexico.

Western USA

Here the nation's most dramatic landscapes can be found. The Rocky Mountains form several large mountain ranges. Vast quantities of powder snow make this one of the world's biggest winter skiing areas, the main centres being

What do the stars and stripes mean on the United States flag?

The flag of the United States has 13 horizontal red stripes, which represent the 13 original colonies. In the top left corner of the flag is a blue rectangle with 50 small, white stars. These represent the 50 states in the United States of America. The flag is known as 'the Stars and Stripes'.

Did the *Mayflower* take the first settlers to America?

No. The first settlers are thought to have been a group of English traders who landed in Virginia in 1607. But the Mayflower, which sailed in 1620, is probably the most famous of the early ships to go to America. Those on board included 102 passengers from Holland and Britain. A replica of the Mayflower can be seen at Plymouth, Massachusetts.

near Aspen in Colorado and Lake Tahoe in California. As the traditional coal, steel and automobile industries of the Eastern USA declined, many people moved to the West Coast where new industries were growing. Aircraft and software development in Seattle, computer component development and manufacture in 'Silicon Valley' San Francisco, and the music, movie and entertainment industries of Los Angeles have built one of the richest regions in the world. Television and film dominate American culture and spread it throughout the world. Hollywood movies are viewed worldwide, as are such long-running television programs as 'The Simpsons'.

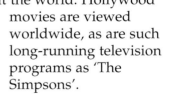

Southern California, Nevada and Arizona are desert, the driest place being in Death Valley. Water from the River

Colorado has cut the deep gorges of the Grand Canyon and Bryce Canyon, and provides much needed water for the farmers and cities of California.

Eastern USA

Europeans have settled the eastern half of the USA since 1613, and many towns are named after the places from which these colonists came. People who migrated to settle permanently in colonies controlled by their country of origin were called colonists or settlers. Sometimes the settlers formed the colony themselves if they settled in an unpopulated area. A colony is the territory where the people settle.

New Orleans

New Orleans, called the Big Easy due to its relaxed life style, is the world's jazz capital, and the Mardi Gras festival attracts millions of visitors. In August 2005, Hurricane Katrina, the largest hurricane ever recorded over the USA, flooded over 80% of New Orleans.

Washington, D.C.

Washington, D.C., named after the first President, George Washington, is the capital city and home to the President of the United States and to the US Capitol. It was designed in 1791 by a French architect and was the world's first planned capital. Washington, D.C., is one of America's most visited sites.

The world's largest silver nugget, weighing 835 kg (1,840 lbs) was found in 1894 near Aspen, Colorado.

Disney World, near Orlando, Florida is the world's largest tourist attraction, covering an area of 12,140 hectares (30,000 acres).

Fascinating Facts

Volcanoes

Deep under the Earth is very hot runny liquid called 'magma'. Sometimes the magma rises to the surface, building up great pressure, and than an eruption occurs. When this happens, a volcano is formed. Gases and lava shoot up through the opening and spill out, causing lava flows, mudslides and falling ash. Large pieces of lava are called lava bombs. An erupting volcano can also cause earthquakes and tsunamis.

Active volcanoes

A volcano is considered 'active' if lava comes out of the top. When this happens, the volcano is 'erupting'. If volcanoes have been quiet for a long time they are 'inactive'. Some inactive volcanoes suddenly become active.

Dormant and extinct volcanoes

Some volcanoes have not erupted for at least 10,000 years. These volcanoes are described as dormant, since they have the potential to erupt again. Some volcanoes only erupt once, and these are called 'extinct', because they will not erupt again.

Cone shapes

The volcano's eruptions can create cone-shaped accumulations of volcanic material. The thickness of the underground magma determines how a volcano will erupt, and what kind of cone will form. There are three cone shapes: cinder cones, shield cones, and stratovolcanoes cones.

Cinder shapes

Cinder cones have straight sides with steep slopes and a large, bowl-shaped crater at the summit. They rarely rise to more than 304 m (1,000 feet) above the surrounding landscape. They are known for their very violent, explosive, exciting eruptions. Paricutin in Mexico is a famous cinder cones.

Shield shapes

Shield cones have very gentle slopes. They were named by Icelandic people because the cones' shape reminded them of a warrior's shield laid down. These volcanoes erupt many times over the same area forming huge, thick lava plateaus. The Columbia Plateau of the western United States is the largest lava plateau in the world. It covers almost 259,000 sq km (100,000 square miles) and is almost a mile thick in places.

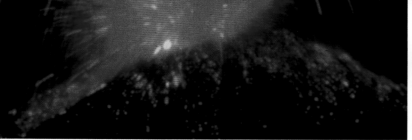

Stratovolcanoes shapes

Stratovolcanoes cones have gentle lower slopes, but steep upper slopes. They are formed from a combination of eruptions. First the volcano has an explosive eruption that ejects huge amounts of steam, gas and ash. This is followed by the ejection of lava. A large cone is built up with many layers of ash and lava. These are the most common volcanic cones, and a famous example is Mount St Helens in Washington.

Underwater volcanoes

Many volcanoes begin on the sea floor. The vast cones of the Hawaiian islands and many other volcanic islands in the Pacific Ocean began like this.

Worst eruptions

There have been many cataclysmic eruptions. After a series of eruptions over the course of several days (26–27 August 1883), the uninhabited island of Krakatoa in Sumatra/ Java exploded with probably the loudest bang ever heard by humans, audible up to 4,800 km (3,000 miles) away. About

How often do you think volcanoes erupt?

Every day, ten volcanoes erupt somewhere on Earth. Most of these are small eruptions, but they may be followed by larger ones.

What is 'The Lighthouse of the Mediterranean'?

Stromboli, off the coast of Italy, has erupted repeatedly over many centuries. The volcano has been called 'The Lighthouse of the Mediterranean' because it erupts every 20 minutes or so.

200,000 people died, most of them killed by subsequent tsunamis with waves up to 30 m (98.5 ft).

When Vesuvius erupted suddenly in 79 AD, the town of Pompeii in Italy was buried under a vast layer of rock and volcanic ash. The town was preserved in a near-perfect state, and uncovered by archeological excavations that began in 1738.

The word volcano comes from the Roman god of fire, Vulcan. Vulcan was said to have had a forge (a place to melt and shape iron) on Vulcano, an active volcano on the Lipari Islands in Italy.

Mauna Loa, Hawaii, is the tallest mountain in the world if measured from the floor of the ocean where it was formed. It is 4165 m (13,677 ft) above sea level, but over 5177 m (17,000 ft) lies under the water. So this volcanic mountain is over 9137 m (30,000 ft) tall!

Fascinating Fact

Water

W ater has the chemical formula H_2O, which means each water molecule is made of two hydrogen atoms and one oxygen atom. Water is the only substance that naturally occurs in solid, liquid and gaseous forms on the Earth.

Water is very important to life. Roughly 97% of the Earth's water is held in the oceans, which cover approximately 70% of the Earth's surface.

How is water vapour important?

Water vapour in the atmosphere is a greenhouse gas – it helps to reduce the amount of heat escaping from the planet into space. If there were no water vapour in the atmosphere the average temperature on the Earth would be –18°C (0.4°F)!

How are polar ice caps important?

The polar ice caps are extremely important to the global climate. They reflect heat more efficiently than the oceans or land and so help to regulate the amount of heat the Earth absorbs from the sun. They also lock away vast quantities of water that would otherwise be part of the oceans – if all the ice in the world were to melt the average sea level would rise by 70 m (230 ft)! (See Global Warming, page 92, for more about this.)

Water has the following physical properties:
- Its freezing point is 0°C (32°F) and its boiling point is 100°C (212°F).
- A litre of water weighs 1 kg (2.2 lbs).
- Its pH is 7, meaning it is neutral (see Acids and alkalis, page 12 for more on this).
- It is an excellent solvent, meaning lots of things, particularly salts, will dissolve very well in it.
- It absorbs more red light (and infra-red) than blue light, so large bodies of pure water appear blue.

The water cycle

- Water in the oceans evaporates as it is heated by the sun's heat, forming water vapour.
- This vapour rises into the atmosphere where it cools and condenses to form clouds of tiny water droplets.
- As these clouds encounter turbulence (rough, windy weather), the tiny water droplets collide and merge into larger droplets.
- These fall as precipitation (rain, sleet, hail or snow).
- This water collects on land into streams and rivers both above and underground. Eventually most of it flows back into the sea, where it will evaporate once more.

Of course, water doesn't always follow the cycle in order – some water will fall directly back into the oceans as rain, and some evaporates from rivers and streams before it gets back to the sea.

How do we use water?

Without water, we would be unable to survive. Industry uses large amounts of water in a variety of ways, including as a coolant in power stations, or as a solvent or chemical agent in many manufacturing and refining processes. Water has many industrial uses, such as irrigation, transportation and power generation.

Irrigation to water the plants

Irrigation is where water from another source (such as a nearby river) is diverted into fields along a series of channels. In some places this is essential to allow crops to be grown at all.

Transportation

Since the invention of boats and ships water has been used to transport goods and people from place to place – first along rivers and later over the seas and oceans. Ships remain a vital component of world trade.

Power generation

Hydroelectric power stations use moving water to turn turbines that generate electricity. There are two basic types – dams and tidal. In a hydroelectric dam a river is blocked by building a large dam across it (causing a reservoir of water to build up behind the dam). The water in the reservoir is at a much higher level than the water on the other side, so when it is allowed to flow it has a lot of force behind it. This force is used to drive the water through a turbine, causing it to spin and generate electricity. In a tidal hydroelectric station the force to drive the turbines comes from the ebb and flow of the tides.

People can usually go without food for weeks if necessary but can only survive for about three days without water.

Every living thing on Earth still needs liquid water to survive. Humans are roughly 70% water and need to drink water regularly to stay healthy.

Fascinating Facts

The wheel

Imagine living in a world without wheels! That's exactly what people did until the Bronze Age. They had no wheeled carts to carry themselves or their things, no machinery run by wheels, and all their pottery was made without that crucial tool, the potter's wheel.

In the Bronze Age, horses and oxen began to be used as 'pulling' animals (we call these 'draft animals') and wheeled carts were developed. People also discovered how to use wheels in making pottery at this time.

The wheel was probably the greatest mechanical invention ever. Nearly every machine ever built – from tiny watch gears to engines and computer disk drives – makes some use of the wheel.

Invention

The earliest known examples of the wheel date from 3,500 BC. They were used in Ancient Mesopotamia and were rather clumsy solid disks of solid wood.

By 2,000 BC the ancient Egyptians were using a more advanced design – they developed spoked wheels to use on their chariots. These were much lighter (so the chariots could go faster), and could be repaired instead of discarded if they got damaged.

What did people use before the wheel?

Before they had wheeled carts, people used to move things by dragging them along. On smooth surfaces like ice and snow, this worked just fine – sledges are still popular forms of transport in cold areas. On rougher ground, though, dragging things was very hard work.

Sometimes logs were cut and used as rollers – heavy items like building blocks could be pushed forward more easily on a bed of rollers.

The potter's wheel

The potter's wheel came into use around 3,500 BC in Mesopotamia. Now potters could easily turn the pot they were making, instead of having to move around it themselves or keep picking it up to turn it.

 **How do we turn a wheel if we can't reach it?**

A shaft or handle can be attached to the axle. Making the axle turn automatically turns the wheel – the wheel itself might be out of reach inside a piece of machinery, but we can still make it turn from outside.

Think about what happens when you push a wheelbarrow – you don't have to touch the wheel to move it. An axle runs through the middle of the wheel. When you push your wheelbarrow, the axle transmits your forward movement to the wheel, which turns.

Uses of the wheel

The waterwheel

The waterwheel uses flowing or falling water to create power. The water hits a set of paddles on the wheel, causing it to turn. The movement energy of the wheel is carried to machinery by the shaft of the wheel.

Spinning wheel

A spinning wheel is a simple machine designed to twist wool or cotton into long lengths of thread. It is usually turned by hand or by a foot pedal. The person working the spinning wheel is called the 'spinster'.

Cogwheel

A cogwheel, or gear wheel, is a toothed wheel that engages with another toothed wheel in order to change the speed or direction of something.

The turbine – a modern waterwheel

The turbine works in a similar way to the waterwheel. A turbine is an engine that uses a fluid (gas or liquid) to drive machinery. Hydraulic, or water, turbines are used to drive electric generators in hydroelectric power stations. They use a flow of liquid to turn a shaft that drives an electric generator.

Having fun with wheels

As well as making our lives much easier, the wheel crops up in many of our leisure activities. Biking, roller-blading and skate-boarding are obvious fun uses of the wheel. We also see it in fairground rides, and even as a spinning firework, the Catherine Wheel.

Fascinating Facts

Some archaeologists think the potter's wheel was actually the first use of the wheel, before wheels were ever put onto carts!

A water wheel was described as early as 4000 BC by a Greek writer.

Zoology

Zoology is the study of animals. The word zoology is taken from 'zoon', the Greek word for animal, and 'logy' meaning to study.

The ancient Greek philosopher Aristotle was one of the first zoologists, but it was not until the Middle Ages that zoology became widely studied. The English scientist Edward Wootton wrote *De differentiis animalium* in 1552. Through his study of Aristotle's earlier work and close observation of nature, Wootton's work extended knowledge about animals.

In Britain the term 'zoology' became well-known through the opening of zoological gardens in the 19th century. The name was soon shortened, and today there are zoos in most big cities. Visitors go there to observe wild animals, though many are in cages. Although the first zoos were intended for the entertainment of visitors, in recent years zoos have also focused on conservation (protecting animals from extinction) and education.

Modern zoos

Modern zoos often keep animals in enclosures designed to be like their natural surroundings. Nocturnal animals, which are only active at night, are seen during the day with dim artificial lighting. At night, when the visitors have gone, the animals are exposed to bright lighting. They think this is daylight, so they rest.

Modern zoos often include children's zoos where children can see, and sometimes touch and feed, domestic animals and certain wild animals. This is especially important for children who live in cities, and rarely visit the countryside or see animals in their natural habitat (living area).

Endangered species

We say that a species (type) of animal is endangered when there are only very few of them still left in the world. We also describe this as being threatened with extinction – this means that the species is under threat of dying out. Some countries have conservation plans to keep endangered animals alive, and boost their numbers. In Florida in the United States there is a Center for Elephant Conservation, opened in 1995, which is a 200-acre sanctuary (resting-place) for retired circus elephants. Dedicated to just one species, this centre has the largest gene pool for the Asian Elephant outside Southeast Asia.

Many animals around the world are in danger of extinction because they have been killed by hunters for their meat, skins, teeth or tusks. Others have lost their natural habitat when forests have been cleared for farming or building. Programmes of breeding these animals in captivity, and sometimes returning them to the wild, are well developed in a number of zoos around the world.

Giant pandas are an endangered species whose numbers have diminished through loss of their natural habitat, and very low birth rate. Although it is very rare for giant pandas to be born in captivity, two cubs were born in different zoos in the US in 2005. A male cub, Tai Shan, was born in July 2005 at the National Zoo in Washington, followed quickly by the birth of a female cub, Su Lin, in August at San Diego Zoo in California.

What is the Ménagerie du Jardin des Plantes?

The Ménagerie du Jardin des Plantes is the first zoo which was created specifically for scientific and educational purposes. It opened in 1794 in Paris, France, and is still open today.

Who is Jing Jing?

Jing Jing is a giant panda and mascot for the 2008 Olympic Games in Beijing, China.

Flags *of the* world

 AFGHANISTAN

 ALBANIA

 ALGERIA

 ANDORRA

 ANGOLA

 ANGUILLA

 ANTIGUA

 ARGENTINA

 ARMENIA

 AUSTRALIA

 AUSTRIA

 AZERBAIJAN

 BAHAMAS

 BAHRAIN

 BANGLADESH

 BARBADOS

 BELARUS

 BELGIUM

 BELIZE

 BENIN

 BERMUDA

 BHUTAN

 BOLIVIA

 BOSNIA & HERZEGOVINA

 BOTSWANA

 BRAZIL

 BRITISH VIRGIN ISLANDS

 BRUNEI

 BULGARIA

 BUKINA FASO

 BURUNDI

 CAMBODIA

 CAMEROON

 CANADA

 CAPE VERDE

 CAYMAN ISLANDS

 CENTRAL AFRICAN REPUBLIC

 CHAD

 CHILE

 CHINA

 COLOMBIA

 COMOROS

 CONGO, DEMOCRATIC REPUBLIC OF

 CONGO, REPUBLIC OF

 COOK ISLANDS

COSTA RICA

COTE D'IVOIRE

CROATIA

CUBA

CYPRUS

CZECH REPUBLIC

DENMARK

DJIBOUTI

DOMINICA

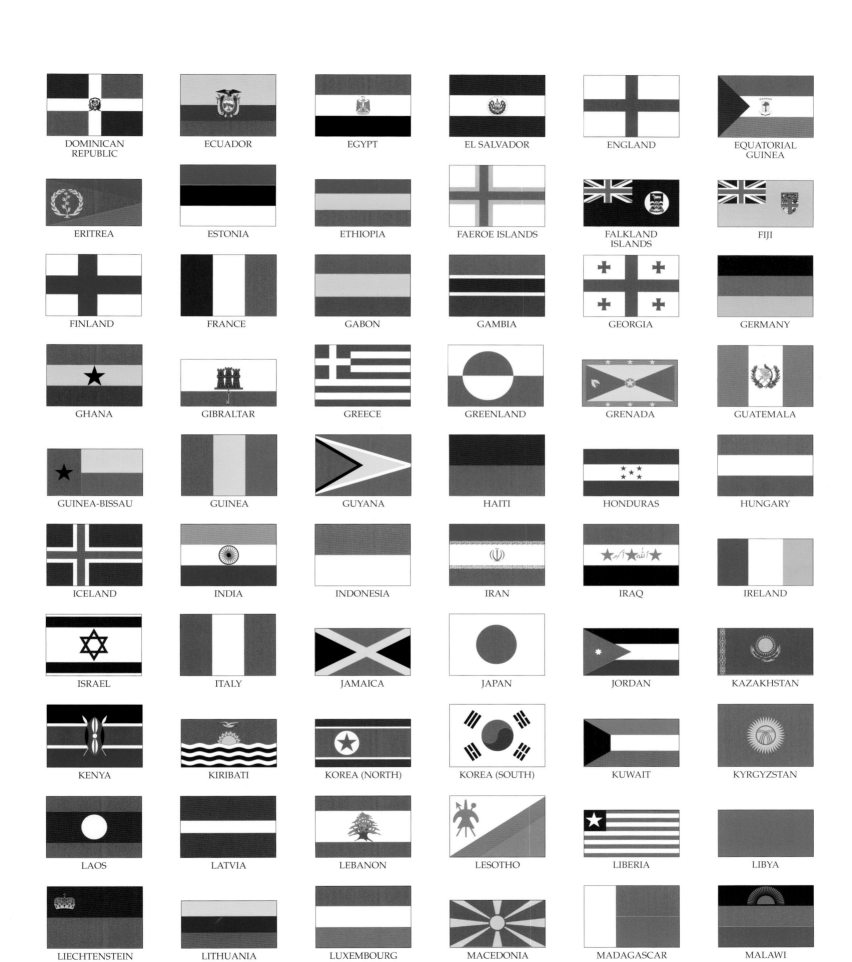

DOMINICAN REPUBLIC

ECUADOR

EGYPT

EL SALVADOR

ENGLAND

EQUATORIAL GUINEA

ERITREA

ESTONIA

ETHIOPIA

FAEROE ISLANDS

FALKLAND ISLANDS

FIJI

FINLAND

FRANCE

GABON

GAMBIA

GEORGIA

GERMANY

GHANA

GIBRALTAR

GREECE

GREENLAND

GRENADA

GUATEMALA

GUINEA-BISSAU

GUINEA

GUYANA

HAITI

HONDURAS

HUNGARY

ICELAND

INDIA

INDONESIA

IRAN

IRAQ

IRELAND

ISRAEL

ITALY

JAMAICA

JAPAN

JORDAN

KAZAKHSTAN

KENYA

KIRIBATI

KOREA (NORTH)

KOREA (SOUTH)

KUWAIT

KYRGYZSTAN

LAOS

LATVIA

LEBANON

LESOTHO

LIBERIA

LIBYA

LIECHTENSTEIN

LITHUANIA

LUXEMBOURG

MACEDONIA

MADAGASCAR

MALAWI

Flags *of the* World

 MALAYSIA

 MALDIVES

 MALI

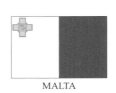 MALTA

 MARSHALL ISLANDS

 MAURITANIA

 MAURITIUS

 MEXICO

 MICRONESIA

 MOLDOVA

 MONACO

 MONGOLIA

 MONTENEGRO

 MONSERRAT

 MOROCCO

 MOZAMBIQUE

 MYANMAR

 NAMIBIA

 NETHERLAND ANTILLES

 NETHERLANDS

 NEW ZEALAND

 NICARAGUA

 NIGER

 NIGERIA

 NAURU

 NEPAL

 NIUE

 NORTHERN IRELAND

 NORWAY

 OMAN

 PAKISTAN

 PANAMA

 PAPUA NEW GUINEA

 PARAGUAY

 PERU

 PHILIPPINES

 POLAND

 PORTUGAL

 PUERTO RICO

 QATAR

 RÉUNION

 ROMANIA

 RUSSIA

 RWANDA

 SAMOA (WESTERN)

 SAN MARINO

 SÃO TOMÉ AND PRINCIPE

 SAUDI ARABIA

 SCOTLAND

 SENEGAL

 SERBIA

 SEYCHELLES

 SIERRA LEONE

 SINGAPORE

SLOVAKIA

SLOVENIA

SOLOMAN ISLANDS

SOMALIA

SOUTH AFRICA

SPAIN

SRI LANKA

ST HELENA

ST KITTS & NEVIS

ST LUCIA

ST PIERRE & MIQUELON

ST CHRISTOPHER

ST VINCENT

SUDAN

SURINAME

SWAZILAND

SWEDEN

SWITZERLAND

SYRIA

TAJIKISTAN

TANZANIA

THAILAND

TOGO

TRINIDAD

TUNISIA

TURKEY

TURKMENISTAN

TURKS & CAICOS

TUVALU

UGANDA

UKRAINE

UNITED ARAB EMIRATES

UNITED KINGDOM

UNITED STATES OF AMERICA

URUGUAY

UZBEKISTAN

VANUATU

VATICAN CITY

VENEZUELA

VIETNAM

VIRGIN ISLANDS

WALES

WESTERN SAMOA

YEMEN

ZAMBIA

ZIMBABWE

General history

BC

c.9000	First walled city founded at Jericho
c.3500	First Chinese cities
c.2500	Use of papyrus by the Egyptians
c.2000	Completion of Stonehenge, England (*see* below)
c.1260	Trojan War
776	First Olympic Games in Greece
753	Foundation of Rome, Italy
c.550	Abacus developed, for counting, in China
509	Roman Republic established
221	Start of the Great Wall of China
c.5	Birth of Jesus

AD

27	Baptism of Jesus
65	Glastonbury Abbey, England, built
105	Paper making started in China
122	Hadrian starts building defensive wall in northern England
350	Gothic Bible produced
350	London, England, fortified
393	Final Olympic Games until modern times held
730	Printing starts in China
787	Vikings attack in Britain
871	King Alfred the Great takes the throne in England
1000	Iron Age settlements in Zimbabwe, Africa
1000	Inca empire growing in south America

1065	Westminster Abbey (above) consecrated (declared a holy place) in London, England
1066	Norman Conquest in England
1086	Domesday Book completed in England
1155	Start of first university in Paris, France
1163	Notre Dame cathedral started in Paris, France
1215	King John signs Magna Carta at Runneymede, England
1290	Spectacles invented
1337	Start of Hundred Years War between England and France
1339	Kremlin constructed in Moscow, Russia
1350	Black Death in Europe
1400	Chaucer dies
1431	Joan of Arc dies
1453	Hundred Years War ends
1445	Gutenberg starts printing in Europe
1475	First book in English printed by Caxton
1509	First watch invented in Germany
1512	Michelangelo finishes painting the Sistine Chapel at the Vatican in Rome, Italy
1521	First books printed in Cambridge, England
1536	England and Wales unify

1558	Elizabeth 1 takes the throne in England
1564	Shakespeare is born
1576	First theatre opens in London, England
1587	Mary, Queen of Scots is killed
1588	England defeats the Spanish Armada
1603	James VI of Scotland inherits the throne of England as James I
1610	Galileo writes about the moons of Jupiter and the rings of Saturn

1610	Tea first imported into Europe from China
1616	Shakespeare dies
1636	Harvard University founded
1638	First printing in America
1642	English Civil War starts
1649	Charles I, King of England, executed
1653	Oliver Cromwell becomes Lord Protector of England
1660	Monarchy restored in England
1660s	Samuel Pepys compiles his diary
1665	Great Plague in London, Britain
1666	Great Fire of London, England
1679	Niagara Falls discovered
1681	First street lamps in London, England
1694	Bank of England established
1701	Yale University founded

1702	First daily newspaper in England circulated
1703	St Petersburg in Russia established
1705	Ships wheel replaces tiller
1710	Christopher Wren completes St Paul's Cathedral (below left) in London
1715	First Jacobite Rebellion in England
1721	Rifle first introduced in America
1741	First iron bridge constructed
1745	Second Jacobite Rebellion
1752	Gregorian calendar started in Britain
1756	Carbon dioxide discovered
1760	Discovery of hydrogen
1764	Invention of steam engine
1771	Discovery of oxygen
1774	Rules of cricket established

1789	Start of French Revolution
1789	George Washington becomes the first president of the USA
1796	Vaccine for smallpox discovered
1800	Act of union between Great Britain and Ireland
1804	Napoleon Bonaparte becomes emperor
1807	Slave trade ended in British Empire
1815	Napoleon defeated at Waterloo
1825	Start of first passenger railway in England
1829	Braille system invented
1832	First railway built in USA
1835	Telegraph system invented in USA
1840	Queen Victoria marries Prince Albert
1851	Great Exhibition takes place in London
1861–65	American Civil War
1865	Abraham Lincoln assassinated
1867	Typewriter invented

KEY FACTS

General history

1876   Invention of telephone
1885   First cars built by Karl Benz in Germany
1887   Pneumatic tyre invented
1889   Eiffel Tower in Paris, France finished
1901   Blood groups discovered
1901   First Nobel prize awarded
1903   First flight by Wright brothers
1908   Model T Ford car (below) first made
1909   First cross-Channel flight between England and France
1912   Titanic sinks
1914-18 First World War in Europe
1917   Russian Revolution
1918   Women in Britain first given limited voting rights
1919   Soviet Republic founded

1919   Atlantic first crossed by air
1920   Start of radio broadcasting
1922   Discovery of tomb of Tutankhamun in Egypt
1926   General Strike in Britain
1926   Early television created
1928   Mickey Mouse is 'born'
1931   Construction of Empire State Building in New York
1933   Polythene invented
1934   Nuclear fission discovered
1936   First television transmissions in Britain
1938   Nylon invented
1938   Ball point pen invented
1939–45 Second World War
1942   First nuclear reactor built
1945   United Nations created
1945   Microwave oven invented
1947   First supersonic flight
1952   Coronation of Elizabeth II in Britain
1953   DNA structure discovered

1956   Video recorder invented
1959   First motorway opened in Britain

1959   Micro chip invented

1963   US President John F. Kennedy assassinated
1963   First woman in space
1967   First heart transplant
1969   First man lands on the moon
1972   Pocket calculator invented

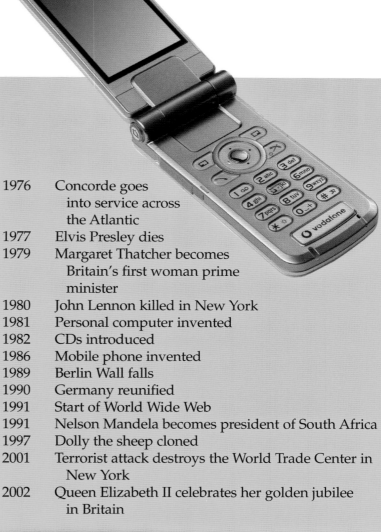

1976   Concorde goes into service across the Atlantic
1977   Elvis Presley dies
1979   Margaret Thatcher becomes Britain's first woman prime minister
1980   John Lennon killed in New York
1981   Personal computer invented
1982   CDs introduced
1986   Mobile phone invented
1989   Berlin Wall falls
1990   Germany reunified
1991   Start of World Wide Web
1991   Nelson Mandela becomes president of South Africa
1997   Dolly the sheep cloned
2001   Terrorist attack destroys the World Trade Center in New York
2002   Queen Elizabeth II celebrates her golden jubilee in Britain

2002   Euro currency introduced
2003   First Chinese astronaut in space
2004   Indian Ocean tsunami hits southern Asia
2005   Hurricane Katrina devastates New Orleans
2005   London awarded 2012 Olympic Games

The world around us

Largest/highest/longest/deepest

The largest lake – Caspian Sea, Iran –
371,000 sq km (143,240 sq miles)

The largest desert – Sahara, North Africa –
8,600,000 sq km (3,320,000 sq miles)

The highest waterfall – Angel Falls, Venezuela –
807 m (2,648 ft)

The longest river – River Nile, North Africa – 6,690 km (4,160 miles)

The highest mountain – Everest, China and Nepal – 8,850 m (29,035 ft)

The largest sea – Coral Sea – 4,791,000 sq km (1,850,200 sq miles)

The largest island – Greenland – 2.175,600 sq km (830,780 sq miles)

The deepest cave – Jean Bernard, France – 1,494 m (4,900 ft)

INDEX

Acknowledgements

The authors and publishers would like to thank the following people
who played such a significant role in creating this Children's Encyclopedia:

Illustration
HL Studios

Page Design
HL Studios

Editorial
Jennifer Clark, Ros Morley, Lucie Williams

Photo research
Ros Morley

Project management
HL Studios

Jacket Design
JPX

Production
Elaine Ward

All photographs are copyright of Jupiterimages.com,
Ros Morley Editing, USGS, NASA, WWF, istockphoto,
stockphoto, stockxchnge, www.imageafter.com, Flickr.com,
except where stated below:

Bayeux Tapestry © GEORGE BERNARD / SCIENCE
PHOTO LIBRARY
Dolly, the world's first adult sheep clone © PH. PLAILLY /
EURELIOS / SCIENCE PHOTO LIBRARY
Artwork of the death of the dinosaurs © D. VAN
RAVENSWAAY / SCIENCE PHOTO LIBRARY
Rodolfo Coria dusting fossil jaw of giant dinosaur ©
CARLOS GOLDIN / SCIENCE PHOTO LIBRARY
Hubble Space Telescope image of the Einstein cross ©
NASA / ESA / STScI / SCIENCE PHOTO LIBRARY
Roman glass jewellery bead, SEM © STEVE
GSCHMEISSNER / SCIENCE PHOTO LIBRARY
Seahorse © Frank Burgey; Aztec Waterway © Ben
Earwicker; Rainforest sunlight © Rolf Esslinger; Totem pole
© Dale Eurenius; Dinosaur bones © Kim Fawcett; Fish
Market Lake Baikal © Enrique Galindo; Bromeliad © Stacy
Graff; Wires Tacoma © Mel Guknes (Singingbarista); Prayer
mat © Alaaeddin Hammoudeh; Helicopter © Dave Johnson
www.tollbarstudio.co.uk; Ford T1 © www.khaane.com;
Ancient Architecture © Marius Largu; Jade mask © Michel
Meynsbrughen (Clafouti); Venus Fly Trap © Dr. David
Midgley, Berowra, NSW, Australia; Waterwheel Arkansas ©
Bill Sarver;